DON'T AWAKEN LOVE
UNTIL IT PLEASES

COMMUNICATING THE SACREDNESS OF SEXUAL
INTIMACY WITH DAUGHTERS

I adjure you, O daughters of Jerusalem, by the gazelles or the does of the field, that you not stir up or awaken love until it pleases.

Song of Solomon 2:7

Debbie Wood and Amanda Clark

P.O. BOX 11893
LEXINGTON, KY 40578

DIVINE APPOINTMENTS PUBLISHING

P.O. BOX 41
ALLARDT, TN 38504

© 2023 Debbie Wood and Amanda J. Clark

All rights reserved. No portion of this book may be reproduced in any form without written permission from the publisher or author, except as permitted by U.S. copyright law. For permission contact amanda@disciplingwomen.com or debbie@familyfortress.org.

Published by:

Divine Appointments Publishing
P.O. Box 41
Allardt, TN 38504

And

Family Fortress Ministries, Inc.
P.O. Box 11893
Lexington, KY 40578

Scripture quotations are from The ESV® Bible (The Holy Bible, English Standard Version®), copyright © 2001 by Crossway, a publishing ministry of Good News Publishers. Used by permission. All rights reserved.

ISBN: 979-8-9875377-2-5

ACKNOWLEDGEMENTS

"Appreciation" seems inadequate when attempting to express our gratitude. There are many that deserve recognition for enabling and encouraging our efforts to see these truths brought together into a complete thought worthy to be shared.

Predominantly, we wish to declare our triune God, as our Creator, our Redeemer, and our Counselor. Maintaining an order of biblical prominence, we must next recognize our devoted husbands. Sam, we thank you for unselfishly acknowledging Debbie's gift of mentoring and teaching. As you allowed for flexibility in her schedule, you have permitted the work that will benefit many for years to come. Wes, we are grateful for your willingness to manage the home-front in Amanda's absence, while she was away working on this project. Your intentional work with the children, especially ensuring Laurel was potty-trained upon her return, was a thoughtful gift!

To the number of ladies who dedicated their time to reading our initial draft—your personal testimonies and feedback inspired us to continue the work. Mrs. Sandra Mullinix and Mrs. Andrea Wood, we appreciate your attention to detail and your eagerness to employ your gift of editing for the glory of God.

FORWARD

    I've always been a curious person, so naturally, I want to know the truth behind things. I was nine when I started to wonder about sex. My parents wanted me to learn the truth about sex from them. They knew that if I didn't get answers quickly, I'd probably try to find them myself.

    I thank God that my parents had godly influences who helped prepare them to share the truth with me. The way my parents talked with me about sex was enlightening. Mom reminds me that my exact response was: "My heart is lightened!" They took me straight to our most reliable source for answers. It was a place they wanted me to grow to trust as I began to seek out truth on my own; they took me to the Bible.

    Before I knew the truth, I noticed I felt guilty about even thinking about the word. How does that even happen? I think we naturally sense it is something of significance, and we begin to draw wrong conclusions when it is not openly discussed. I believe that every girl should learn about sex from a biblical perspective. I have friends who don't understand that God created it to be beautiful and pure. I hate to see that their understanding of sex is so distorted.

    This is a much-needed tool for moms, and daughters alike, to know there is a welcoming way to begin talking about sex. We need to see it as the good thing that God created it to be.

Thankful for Truth,
Macy, Age 15

Contents

INTRODUCTION	13
"How Do I Tell My Daughter?"	13
CHAPTER ONE	17
S-E-X	17
CHAPTER TWO	27
Breaking Tradition	27
CHAPTER THREE	37
Purpose Brings Peace	37
CHAPTER FOUR	43
A Pathway for Parents	43
CHAPTER FIVE	49
Recipe for Romance	49
CHAPTER SIX	65
Private Property	65
CHAPTER SEVEN	77
Neighborhood Watch	77
CHAPTER EIGHT	87
Repurpose Regret	87
CONCLUSION	95
God's Endorsement	95

EPILOGUE 99
Awaken, My Love! 99
Appendix A 115
Multiple Dating Relationships 115
Character Considerations in a Future Mate 116
Conquering Insecurities 117
Appendix B 121
Release from Sexual Bondage 121
Appendix C 123
Living It Out in the Home 123
Submission 123
Appendix D 125
Mother-Daughter Activities 125
Appendix E 129
Awaken Resources 129

INTRODUCTION

"How Do I Tell My Daughter?"

I have four sons. Why in the world would I attempt to encourage moms with thoughts on how to explain sexual intimacy to their young daughters? Obviously not because I have experience. It is because of all the questions:

> "My nine-year-old daughter was innocently building castles at the sandbox when a friend started elaborating incorrect crude detail about sexual intimacy. She came to me, horrified and scared. I am thankful she came to me, but how do I straighten this out for her? "

> "My husband and I are expecting another baby and our daughter is asking questions and wanting more information. I feel like someone has been filling her in on things I do not think she was ready to hear. Help!!!!"

> "My daughter is getting to "that age." Do you have any resources to equip me to explain sex in a way that displays its beauty and sacredness?"

We repeatedly get questions like this at our resource table, at church, through our counseling and through emails. So, I searched for resources for these moms, but never found one that used the scriptures to prepare young girls for the precious future God has for them when they one day get married. The need was so compelling for one mom, Amanda, who is now my co-author, that she asked to come to my house so that we could process through key scriptures addressing the topics of sex and purity. She wanted some direction and insight as she approached the subject with her daughter. A few days after we spent that afternoon examining God's sacred and fulfilling plan, she called back because she felt as though all of her friends were also at a point where they needed to lay these truths out for their own daughters. This resulted in a Bible study with a group of her friends and these notes were born out of her urgency to share truth.

The goal is to equip moms with biblical explanations of marriage and physical intimacy so they can work with their daughters to develop a positive, respectful, and sacred attitude towards sex. Our desire is that more and more moms will become emboldened to embrace discussions on S-E-X because they are saturated in truth.

This is a process, almost a lifetime of conversations, in which the information needs to be adjusted to fit the maturity of the child and then expanded as she grows in understanding. In every conversation, whether planned or impromptu, whether casual or an actual scripture lesson, God and His ways should be exalted. We believe this removes fear and inspires a respect for marriage and a confident passion to live life according to God's plan. We pray our Father, the designer of physical intimacy, will use the truths in this book to develop precious bonds that give daughters freedom to trust both their parents and their heavenly Father.

Each chapter begins from the perspective of a mother desiring instruction. You will see how her concerns are addressed, using scripture and explanations that equip her to point her child to God's truth. The first chapter expounds basic principles that are foundational and important for each stage of a child's development, including very young ages. Although the text in the explanations of scripture begin in the early chapters with language understandable for younger children and increases in age-level appropriateness both in wording and intensity of the subject, a mother will still need to expound these foundational principles to teens before advancing to the later more detailed chapters. The text is not a script—but rather information for a mother to process and convey as needed and as age appropriateness allows. Make sure you read the footnotes. They contain valuable information to use as your daughter matures or asks questions.

Before we dig into explanations of scripture, we want to offer a few tips and thoughts to keep in mind:

- Start explaining marriage at a young age. As your child matures, expand into the physical privileges of husband and wife.
- With every explanation, remind your daughter she can come to you and ask questions because you will never judge her, but will always tell her the truth.
- Open your Bible and read the account as you explain. For toddlers, use a Bible story book[1] and supplement with explanations, but always let your daughter know all of this is in the Bible; therefore, she can know it is right and true.
- Repeatedly affirm these truths in everyday life—adding detail as needed.
- Know it and live it well so when casual conversation allows, you can reinforce or even introduce different aspects. Remember, you can address any question with confidence as long as you go back to God's Word. See Appendix C for resources to help you as an adult embrace and live these truths.
- In the New Testament, when Jesus and Paul addressed marriage or sexual relations, they consistently cited the first marriage relationship; so always start at creation. As your daughter matures and you expand the details, remind her that the plan originated at creation.

---

[1] *Jesus Storybook Bible* by Sally Lloyd Jones. Our favorite bible storybook for 5-9 year olds. *Beginners Gospel Bible Storybook* is an excellent choice for toddlers.

- Read the scriptures as you work your way through the chapters and don't forget the footnotes.

CHAPTER ONE

S-E-X
Seeking to Embrace Sex:
The Not-So-Typical Sex Talk

"S-E-X" evokes a negative connotation these days. Honestly, just typing out the letters brings up a natural cautionary flag in this momma's heart. I bet it does the same for many of you. If it didn't, you probably would not have been drawn to this book. It is natural, healthy, and biblical to be cautious when approaching this subject. I believe that God has placed His Spirit within us to help us discern topics such as this. He knew that our sin nature would have a tendency to misuse what He created and, therefore, gave us clear boundaries to help us follow His perfect plan. Consequently, it is no different for sex.

Much of the "caution" that I personally feel is rooted in fear. Fear is defined by Merriam-Webster as *"an unpleasant emotion caused by the belief that someone or something is dangerous, likely to cause pain, or a threat."* There are likely many reasons that we fear these conversations. The enemy has been widely successful in taking what God created and turning it into something ugly. It is probably no surprise to you that he also will not stop short of his attempt to shut down all healthy communication regarding sex.

My daughter approached me after a youth group service one evening. She had noticed that while the youth pastor spoke about sex, many of the young girls seemed extremely nervous. She had consequently noticed that she did not feel embarrassed. This led her to question herself, and she came to me wondering if it was wrong that she was not made uncomfortable by the discussion. Most likely, these girls were truly anxious during this talk. Whether the reason was that it had been a taboo discussion in their homes or, maybe even worse, it had been misused around them, they were noticeably anxious. I must acknowledge that the reason my daughter was not grieved by this discussion was only because of God's grace. God has given us many opportunities to have healthy, open discussions guided by the principles we are sharing with you in the chapters that follow.

However, our ability to embrace these conversations, did not come easily. There was also a time, at a younger age, when my daughter was frightened at the term "sex." It is everywhere! "Big and Sexy" hair products, "What sex (gender) are you?" and "May cause sexual dysfunction." are just a few of the awkward conversation starters we encountered. She even went as far as to leave her Sunday School class in a panic anytime she heard the word. Sunday School should have been a safe place for her to approach the subject. Yet, because of a previous distorted initial exposure, she was uncomfortable, even terrified.

Her confusion led me to seek out Godly counsel in preparation for "The Talk." There is no hard standard for when this talk should occur. Actually, we believe that it should not be just a one-time "talk" at all. It is a conversation that should begin as early as the toddler years and should allow you to go more in depth as necessary or, at least, as bodies begin to transition through puberty. Remember, all kids are different. We cannot rely on a perfect formula. Some may, out of curiosity, initiate these conversations often while others may be too embarrassed to approach an adult with their questions. Most importantly, we encourage you not to wait until hormones are raging, and your children have found out through experience. If left to this path of knowledge, it will, no doubt, be a flawed, perverted, and untrue picture of God's amazing design.

Our God is a God of details. Sometimes it is the details that overwhelm us. I urge you not to skip over the very intimate particulars. It is in those specifics where His glory is revealed, and the beauty of His plan is highlighted. Embrace His Word as your guide. It will not fail you.

You may be thinking, "Did I read correctly? Did you really advise me to start these conversations with a toddler? What in the world should I tell a toddler? Where do I start? How do I know what to say?" Feeling stressed? I felt such relief when I realized God has already laid the lesson out for us. As a matter of fact, it is foundational and is the starting point, no matter the age.

As It Was in the Beginning

The beginning is always a great place to start. Many of us feel an increase in anxiety when we recognize the conversation is heading towards the topic of sex. The opportunities are many and can range from "Where do babies come from?" to "What is a crush?" to "Why are those two men holding hands?" We encourage you to take advantage of every question and intentionally prepare your responses.

God laid the foundation for us in the first book of the Bible. Genesis is the perfect place to see His heart for His creation and to learn about His plans for man and woman. These truths are what everything else builds upon.

When and how should you begin these conversations? We recommend as soon as possible; as soon as you begin teaching your child that God is Creator. He initiated marriage with the first man and woman He created.

The truths in God's Word are not rated by the age of the audience. They are always appropriate where they can be applied. Pray for guidance and allow the Holy Spirit to direct you. Let's BEGIN!

Genesis 1:29-30

And God said, "Behold, I have given you every plant yielding seed that is on the face of all the earth, and every tree with seed in its fruit. You shall have them for food. And to every beast of the earth and to every bird of the heavens and to everything that creeps on the earth, everything that has the breath of life, I have given every green plant for food." And it was so.

Our wise, loving Father created a perfect, glorious environment where man could thrive. He provided everything Adam needed—food, a beautiful place to live, pleasure and purpose. His job was to take care of the garden. God was Adam's friend. He came every day and talked and walked with Adam. The world was perfect. No danger, no sadness, no hurts. God's love was evident everywhere.

Genesis 2:15

The LORD God took the man and put him in the garden of Eden to work it and keep it.

Adam was busy enjoying what God had given Him. He was living what God planned for Him.

Genesis 2:16-17

And the LORD God commanded the man, saying, "You may surely eat of every tree of the garden, but of the tree of the knowledge of good and evil you shall not eat, for in the day that you eat of it you shall surely die."

Adam had freedom to live life to the fullest. In all of his freedom and pleasure, he needed to continue to show respect and honor to His Maker. He showed honor by obeying the one command God had given Him. God gave the restriction in order to protect Adam because life gets distorted and confusing when we do things our way. We honor God with our obedience because He is God, and He is always right.

Genesis 2:18-20

Then the LORD God said, "It is not good that the man should be alone; I will make him a helper fit for him." Now out of the ground the LORD God had formed every beast of the field and every bird of the heavens and brought them to the man to see what he would call them. And whatever the man called every living creature, that was its name. The man gave names to all livestock and to the birds of the heavens and to every beast of the field. But for Adam there was not found a helper fit for him.

In *Genesis* 1-2, as God was creating the world, He looked at what He had done and repeatedly declared that "it is good." Tim Keller notes, "It is striking, then, that after God created the first man, He said, 'It is *not* good that man should be alone.'"[2]

God had made man in His image—not to be another god, but to be a person who thinks, loves, and connects with others. God had not yet provided another human for man to love and talk to and enjoy life with. Adam had all the animals, but they were not like him. He could hug them and play with them, but when they walked by him in pairs to get their names, God made him realize there was no one else like him—another human being. Mr. Rhino had Mrs. Rhino. Mr. Zebra could walk beside Mrs. Zebra and know he belonged. When Mr. Orangutan grabbed a vine to swing across the garden, Mrs. Orangutan clapped for him. No one clapped for Adam. There was no companion comparable to him. God providentially ordained the naming of the animals at this time, so that Adam would recognize the void in his life and be prepared to appreciate the precious gift God had planned for him.

Genesis 2:21-22

So the LORD God caused a deep sleep to fall upon the man, and while he slept took one of his ribs and closed up its place with flesh. And the rib that the LORD God had taken from the man he made into a woman and brought her to the man.

---

[2] Tim Keller, *The Meaning of Marriage* (New York: Dutton, 2011), 110.

Then God took the final steps to complete His plan for creation. He made exactly what Adam needed, a helper companion—specially designed for him. This helper[3] would enable and empower him to do what God had designed him to do. This was God's plan from the very beginning. The words, *made a woman*, mean the Creator artistically built or fashioned Eve to be exactly what Adam needed. She was the one and only girl for him. Emotionally, she would make him happy. They would share their hearts with each other. They would laugh together. They would encourage each other.

The woman was a precious gift from God. Every wife is a special gift to her husband. He should not get lonely because they can do everything together—eat, walk, talk, fix up a house, plan vacations, laugh, play, work, and raise a family. After creating Eve, God called His creation—very good! Man was no longer alone; creating both man and woman for each other was the highlight of His creation!

Genesis 2:23

Then the man said, "This at last is bone of my bones and flesh of my flesh; she shall be called Woman, because she was taken out of Man."

When God brought the woman to Adam, he could not believe his eyes. There was someone just like him. He would never be lonely again. He was so delighted he sang a song about her.

Genesis 2:24

Therefore a man shall leave his father and his mother and hold fast to his wife, and they shall become one flesh.

---

[3] The Hebrew word used in v 18 for helper is *ezer*. This is a glorious view of a wife's role because *ezer* is one of the Hebrew descriptions of God Himself often found in the Psalms—a very present *help* in time of need; God is our *help* and shield. It means one who empowers and enables. God specifically fashioned woman to empower and enable her husband to fulfill God's will for his life. She was designed to fit (correspond to his specific needs—emotionally and physically). Without her, man experiences a void; that is, he is lonely, missing something in life. A wife is a unique precious gift to her husband.

Adam and Eve got married and became a family. This was God's precious plan. But this plan was not just for Adam and Eve. He planned some people would remain single (*1 Corinthians* 7:8-9); but that most of the time, a man would grow up and leave his parents and join together with his wife to start a new family unit.

God intended that the husband would protect his wife and make sure she had food and a place to live. Most of all, he would love her. He designed the woman to be a companion, a partner so the husband would not get lonely. God wanted her to cooperate with her husband and help him take care of their home. Best of all, they would worship God together. They could do things God's way and be secure forever.

In this verse, God says a man will leave his parents and *cleave* or *hold fast* or *join tightly* to his wife. The word means to make a covenant or a promise to be inseparable. They would stick together like glue. In our culture a couple makes this promise when they exchange marriage vows. This means Adam and Eve and every bride and groom promise to be companions forever.[4] Marriage is a covenant (promise) of companionship between a man and a woman (*Malachi* 2:14)[5]. Once a couple makes this promise to be companions, they live together and show their love by hugging and kissing. Hugging her husband tightly reminds a wife he is her one and only man. God intends the husband be the most important man in the world to a wife. They belong to each other forever. This is enough explanation for a toddler; but as the toddler's understanding and awareness increase, a more in-depth explanation of one flesh should be introduced.

---

[4] The word cleave means to unite to someone through a covenant, a binding promise, or oath (Deuteronomy 10:20). The explanation for cleave is powerfully explained by Keller:
Tim Keller, *The Meaning of Marriage,* 82-83.
[5] Sam and Debbie Wood, *What is Marriage?,* (Jamestown, TN: Family Fortress Ministries, 2016), 24.

The words *one flesh* express the idea that the couple is so connected with each other they become one unit like a specialized team. They fit together[6].

God even designed their bodies to fit together and move together. A man is hairy and has a lot of muscles, but a woman is soft and curvy. So, after they make their promises in front of God (get married), the husband and wife can snuggle up and it will feel so good. This helps them love each other even more.

Starting with Adam and Eve, this has always been God's plan—that a husband and wife promise to take care of each other and to serve Him together forever. They belong to each other.

Tim Savage wonderfully expands the meaning of *one flesh* in a way that will enhance a teen's view of the sacredness and seriousness of marriage:

> In the Bible, the word flesh is used to describe what a person is at the core of his or her being. Hence when two people become one flesh, they unite at the deepest level. They become, as it were, ontologically one. Such a dramatic union represents far more than the sum of shared interests or the bond of sexual intimacy. It is a fusion of souls, an organic commingling of two individual lives. Husbands and wives are no

---

[6] Clasp your hands as you explain fit together. This paints a mental picture of physically joining and lays the groundwork for future conversation about fitting together. As the child matures you can describe fitting together or cleaving as a puzzle that joins together. What an amazing design! Only God would plan that. This act is very natural for kids who grow up around animals. When they comment on an animal couple that is mating, this is a perfect opportunity to go back to this verse and talk about God's design of fitting together. It is another opportunity to later explain that homosexuality does not fit God's design. The body parts do not fit the way He planned. God gave man a woman to be his specialized companion.

Anatomy books will be a great resource as the child breaks into puberty. No need to be awkward. Just keep expressing amazement at God's design. He designed a husband and wife's body to respond to gentle touch by changing to fit together even better. Your explanation can be expanded to say the bodies fit so well together that they can join and move like one person.

longer two apart but one together. Like the fusion of a sperm and an egg, they become a new organism. The fusion does not dissolve their original personalities but redirects those personalities toward each other in such a way that the best traits of each spill out into the other.[7]

Embracing God's design for one flesh in marriage will serve to fortify a young woman's heart to trust the plan of God enough to wait for and marry a man who follows His ways.

---

[7] Tim Savage, *No Ordinary Marriage,* (Wheaton, Illinois: Crossway Books, 2012), 92.

CHAPTER TWO

Breaking Tradition

    Centuries of brokenness, sin, and rebellion have intensified the awkwardness that rises up within every one of us at the mention of "sex." We don't talk about it in our circle of friends. We hush it whenever we can. We rarely even hear it discussed in our churches. We certainly don't wish to discuss it openly in our homes! Or do we? Did you realize most inquisitive young people choose to seek answers to questions on sex from Google rather than from their parents?[8]

    In the past, as I've I reached out to others to share my concerns with them, I was deeply saddened at the response. Many parents today appear to be content ignoring this topic altogether.

    I'm sure you've heard, "Ignorance is bliss." Choosing not to think, or talk, about something may bring relief. However, it is dangerous and it can leave a door open for us to become satisfied walking in darkness.

    I recently read a blog from Proverbs 31 Ministries where the well-known blogger shared her disgust at learning the nutritional values of her favorite pumpkin muffin (I can totally relate!). The Bible does tell us that being informed can cause us some grief. *Ecclesiastes*

---

[8] Why public health scholars should study pornography (theconversation.com) and Parents Need to Talk About Porn (axis.org)

1:18 says "For in much wisdom is much vexation, and he who increases knowledge increases sorrow."

The amount of calories in that muffin was not what she wanted to hear! She would no longer be able to enjoy it the same way as she once had. Now that she was informed, she had a decision to make: would she ignore the truth or accept the responsibility that came along with being given this information?

When we are informed of what our children are thinking or experiencing, it can alarm us. It can sting. Regardless of the unpleasantness encompassing this information, we must have settled in our heart to take full advantage of the moment to share truth with grace. We want to be careful not to shame or unintentionally abandon our children to search for explanations in the corruptness of culture simply because of our discomfort or unpreparedness.

If asked, I do not think that these moms would outwardly admit that they would prefer their children just learn about sex from their friends at school. But if left alone and ignored, that is exactly what will happen! We are fools to believe that our children are not being exposed at school, in books and movies, on social media, etc. They are inundated with sexual content, most likely on a daily basis. That should grieve us. If we are honest, we would admit that we were also "informed" (or rather, misinformed) outside of our homes.

Rather than allow the discouragement to paralyze me, I attempted to find those who shared a similar burden to equip their daughters with the truth. It was evident that many of the moms I spoke with were also clueless as to how to have these conversations — clueless and anxious. The common thread, which I noticed, was-the way it had been told to us.

My intention is not to bring harm or speak negatively about anyone. I do not place blame on any one person for years of faulty discussions (or lack thereof). However, I do desire to shed light on what has become a "murky" subject. In order to get a clearer view, sometimes, it requires bringing them into the light. I recognize the enemy is the father of all lies (*John* 8:44) and would much prefer this subject remain taboo under the cover of darkness. Again, we must consider the number of years in which these lies have been allowed to become mutated from the truth. A common and, seemingly, harmless example of this is how we refer to the sex talk as "The Birds and the Bees." Our intentions may be good, but nothing can appropriately substitute for the real beauty of the intimacy that God created for man and woman.

As an aside, I encourage you to ask your closest friends, or even your own mother, how they were informed about sex. Some testimonies that have been shared with me are:

> "My mom didn't talk with me about sex. I gleaned what I knew at school, from friends."

> "My mom simply said, 'If you do it, it will kill me.'"

> "My mom told me sex was bad and that you don't do it."

If I had to guess, I bet these examples are not much different from how you were told. I realize that these moms (our moms) were probably uninformed themselves. They were just doing what had been modeled to them. That is what we do as humans. We model behaviors; we follow traditions.

It seems that so often, in following suit, we attempt to use guilt-based tactics to convince our children to obey God's Word. Legalism and rules will not produce genuine obedience. These are very short-lived, and both are more likely to stir up rebellion within our flesh. God, Himself, knew our nature would fight against "laws." I believe that is why He showed us what is really needed is a heart change.

Christ desires we trust Him rather than the comfort of tradition. He wants us to break the worldly mold, and He equips us to do just that. It can start with our generation. Our children can become a bold generation that embraces truth and the freedom to discuss the beauty of sex the way it was originally created by God. They can do this because God will direct our conversations; and He will dwell in the midst of our explanations, which are ultimately His. We can pray that their hearts will grow in a desire to follow God's plan, with no shame, because it is good. Mary Kassian, in her book *Girls Gone Wise,* gives us a bold thought:

> Given the modern-day obsession with sex, I'm going to say something that may sound radical: We don't make as much of sex as we should.... The problem is not that we value sex too much-but that we don't value it enough.[9]

The remainder of the chapter expounds God's description of sexual intimacy in an attempt to assign the value it deserves in a way young children can understand, then intensifies for explanations as our daughters grow in maturity.

Naked and Not Ashamed

Genesis 2:25
And the man and his wife were both naked and were not ashamed.

The first husband and wife lived in a perfect environment, enjoying God and creation. Tasty food. Beautiful flowers and trees. Babbling brooks. Cute, gentle animals. No bad thoughts. Total acceptance. No fear. No shame. No guilt.

They talked together about the greatness and goodness of God. They talked to Him and walked with Him. That's why it is important for mommy and daddy to read their Bibles and pray together

---

[9] Mary Kassian, *Girls Gone Wise in a World Gone Wild,* (Chicago, Illinois: Moody Publishers, 2010), 135.

every day.[10] That is our way of communicating with God together.

This verse describes their relationship as naked and not ashamed.[11] There was no bad or evil. Adam and Eve knew only good. The first couple did not laugh at each other or think anything was strange. They only said kind sweet words and continually reminded each other about what an amazing God they served. They did not have secrets. They could tell each other everything because they did not make fun or embarrass one another. Adam and Eve did not need to wear clothes in front of each other because there were no ugly thoughts. This was God's perfect plan for husbands and wives. Besides, the weather in the Garden of Eden was perfect, so the couple did not need clothes to keep warm.

Private nakedness between a husband and wife is acceptable. It's God's plan for closeness. They can hug each other and keep warm.[12] He likes for them to kiss and make each other happy.[13]

Genesis 3:1-4
*Now the serpent was more crafty than any other beast of the field that the L*ORD *God had made. He said to the woman, "Did God actually say, 'You shall not eat of any tree in the garden'?" And the woman said to the serpent, "We may eat of the fruit of the trees in the garden, but God said, 'You shall not eat of the fruit of the tree that is in the midst of the garden, neither shall you touch it, lest you die.'" But the serpent said to the woman, "You will not surely die."*

---

[10] Having daily devotions is key for mom and dad. This strengthens their relationship as they live out this truth before their children. Reinforces God's plan to children. *Time for Three* by Sam and Debbie Wood is a resource with a daily devotion for couples to read together.

[11] The wording implies both a physical and emotional nakedness. Adam and Eve had freedom and did not hide anything from one another. They were completely known, yet still loved and accepted. After sin entered the world, they covered up physically and emotionally because they feared if the other knew the truth they would no longer be loved and accepted. That's shame. It hinders communication and splinters relationships.

[12] Clasp hands again.

[13] It's extremely important to demonstrate appropriate affection towards your husband in front of your children. Let them see the two of you hug and kiss. This gives them security and reinforces God's word for family life.

Since God is the creator, He is the rightful ruler of the universe. We should honor and obey Him. He made us and gave us everything we need so we would be so thankful that we joyfully do whatever He says. It is important that we respect Him and do what He says just because He is God.

God gave Adam and Eve a world of good provisions, but He also gave them one rule. Since He had been so good to them, they should trust him and willingly do the one thing he asked. But the sneaky devil, in the form of a serpent, came to trick Adam and Eve. He shifted their thoughts away from how good God is and got them to think about the fruit God told them not to eat.

They had lots and lots of delicious fruit they could eat, but Satan wanted them to pay more attention to him than to God. He wanted control over them.

So, he lied. He twisted the truth of God. He told Eve she would not die if she ate the fruit. He convinced her she should ignore God and do things his way. He challenged her to consider all the inviting aspects of the fruit.

Genesis 3:5-6
"For God knows that when you eat of it your eyes will be opened, and you will be like God, knowing good and evil." So when the woman saw that the tree was good for food, and that it was a delight to the eyes, and that the tree was to be desired to make one wise, she took of its fruit and ate, and she also gave some to her husband who was with her, and he ate.

The devil made Eve think that if she ate the forbidden fruit, she would be like God, because then she would know good and evil. Up to this point, Eve had only experienced good. All her thoughts were right and true and fulfilling. She had never participated in evil. Who wants to know evil? That makes us sad and selfish and confused.

But when the conniving serpent distracted Eve, she ignored everything God had told her husband and everything God had done for them. Then she started thinking about how much she wanted that fruit and what it would do for her. The selfishness deep in her heart surfaced. Mary Kassian explains, "Eve fell into the trap of thinking that she had the right to judge the merits of the forbidden fruit for herself, rather than simply take God at His word."[14]   The more she thought about how exciting it would be to be like God, she convinced herself to eat and get her husband to disobey and eat too.

When we consider reasons to do things our way, we end up disobeying God. Then sad and bad things happen. Our happiness dies. Life gets distorted and confusing.

When Adam and Eve disobeyed God, everything in the world changed, just like God warned it would. Plants and animals started to die. People became selfish and mean. Sin broke the whole world. God's creation is still amazing, but it is not perfect anymore. Corruption entered. Now Adam and Eve could catch colds, get sick, and eventually die. Diseases started infecting people. Their bodies got aches and pains and started to die. Worst of all, they died spiritually. Because of sin, humans lost their perfect connection with God. There was a death to the unity between man and their God. This brokenness gave way to confusion—"confusion about the nature of God, confusion about God's commands, and confusion about who they were."[15]

Genesis 3:7
Then the eyes of both were opened, and they knew that they were naked. And they sewed fig leaves together and made themselves loincloths.

Now, they knew evil. Before disobedience, man only knew good happy things. Now, they were embarrassed. They started thinking mean and ugly thoughts about each other. Adam and Eve knew they were naked, so they covered up with leaves which is certainly not

---

[14] Kassian, *Girls Gone Wise in a World Gone Wild,* 17.
[15] Gary Steward, *Rejoicing in God's Good Design* (Phillipsburg, New Jersey: P&R Publishing, 2022), V.

adequate clothing. There is nothing bad about bodies—sin and evil thoughts make it necessary to wear clothes.[16]

Mary Kassian expounds the sudden urgency to wear clothes:

> The ugliness in her heart made her (Eve) feel physically ugly. For the first time ever, she felt unattractive. Imperfect. Flawed. Self-conscious…. So she tried to conceal the gap between what she was and what she should have been by covering her most intimate, vulnerable parts with leaves…Nothing could hide the dishonor, disgrace, and embarrassment of their rebellion against their Creator. They could not conceal the fact that they no longer measured up to who He created them to be. [17]

Man changed, but God did not change. Man started thinking selfish thoughts and He was afraid of God, but God remained the same. He continued to love Adam and Eve. He told them about His plan to send someone to rescue their hearts from all their evil thoughts and deeds. Then He used animal skins to make them clothes that would not crumble up and blow away in the wind. God made sure Adam and Eve were covered—so they would not have to be embarrassed and afraid of God and one another. Kassian says:

> The shame of their fallen condition demanded a covering, not to conceal it, but to confess and redeem it. This is a very important point. Clothing bears witness to the fact that we have lost the glory and beauty of our original sin-free selves. It confesses that we need a covering—His covering—to atone for our sin and alleviate our shame. It testifies to the fact that God

---

[16] *God Made All of Me* by Justin Holcomb is and invaluable resource to train children how to protect their bodies from sexual assault. The book emphasizes how our bodies are wonderful and amazing and need to be protected.
[17] Kassian, Mary, *Girls Gone Wise in a World Gone Wild*, 98-99.

solved the problem of shame permanently and decisively with the blood of His own Son.[18]

The problem is man kept on doing things his way. We humans still have a natural tendency to ignore our Heavenly Father and do things our way. This rebellion is a rejection of God and His rightful authority. God's verdict against sin remains the same; the punishment is still death. In the Old Testament, God directed His people to practice ceremonies to kill innocent animals so they would remember and understand the wages of sin is death. The innocent animal without any flaws did not deserve to die. It would die the undeserved death in order to settle the debt owed to God by the person who had sinned. This ceremony was a picture, a foreshadowing, of the death of the innocent, flawless Lamb of God—Jesus Christ, the Son of God.

Because they kept sinning, people had to perform these ceremonies over and over again until the rescuer (Jesus) came to take the punishment they deserved to completely pay the price for how bad they were. He was the Son of God who never did anything wrong but performed God's law perfectly. He sacrificed Himself by dying on the cross so that anyone who depends on Him and Him alone would no longer be separated from God but could become a part of God's family. His sacrifice was complete. It fully satisfied God's wrath once and for all so no more animal sacrifices were needed. Jesus is the promise God made when Adam and Eve sinned.

God's love did not change. He was such a kind God that He let Adam and Eve live for a time before they physically died. He allowed them to have a family just as He had planned.

---

[18] Kassian, Mary, *Girls Gone Wise in a World Gone Wild,* 99.

CHAPTER THREE

Purpose Brings Peace

Proverbs 16:22 tells us, "Good sense is a fountain of life to him who has it, but the instruction of fools is folly." *Benson Commentary* reaffirms, "A clear understanding and right judgement of things, like an inexhaustible spring, gives perpetual comfort and satisfaction to him (her) who has it and makes him (her) very useful unto others."[19] I have been blessed to witness this firsthand. When my daughter had been wrongly informed about sex, she was terribly afraid of it. Something as simple as a tv commercial disclosing that *sex could be dangerous* due to the possible side effects of a particular drug, sent her running to us. That night, my husband and I took our Bible and followed the scriptures just as we have mapped out for you.

Were details necessary? Yes. Did we have to draw out mental pictures for her? Yes. Was it uncomfortable? No. When I saw the relief in her countenance, I was so grateful that my husband made certain there was no room for confusion.

I had lived in fear of having this conversation with her for years. I had done everything possible to avoid any exposure that might bring it up sooner than I had desired. As parents, it is our responsibility to shelter our kids from certain things in life.

---

[19] *Proverbs 16 Benson Commentary.*
https://biblehub.com/commentaries/benson/proverbs/16.htm

Nevertheless, avoidance is not beneficial to anyone. Being a shelter for our children should not mean that we never allow them out to see the light of day. Rather, we should allow them some healthy encounters while providing them a safe place to come back to for wisdom and discernment. This helps them grow in confidence instead of cowering under the pressures from a lack of understanding.

I will never forget how she expressed her relief as we described God's plan for sex. "My heart is lightened!" she said with a sigh. Yes, we wept as we watched her carefree childhood naivety fade into a more mature awareness. Amazingly, our sadness turned to hope, and her anxiety transformed into peace as she began to understand that God created sex and His plan for it was good.

Since the beginning of Creation, we have coveted knowledge. Although the desire for knowledge became sinful when sought through disobedience to God, it was a desire placed there by our Creator.[20] Not only did He create us with a capacity for knowledge, but He also gave us a longing for His truth.

There is freedom in truth (*John* 8:32). If Satan has succeeded in deceiving us, we live in bondage. He knows that he can have no power over us if we live in truth. Parents have the unique opportunity to point their children to the truth and, therefore, steer them away from darkness.

The truth also has a unique way of creating bonds as trust grows. When we are able to provide answers that can be traced back to God's Word, we can be confident we are building a strong connection not only between us and our children, but also between them and their Creator. I think of this bond as being similar to that which was sealed upon Adam and Eve's first sacred union.

---

[20] *Colossians 3 Barnes' Notes.*
https://biblehub.com/commentaries/barnes/Colossians/3.htm

The Intimacy of Knowing

Genesis 4:1
Now Adam knew Eve his wife, and she conceived and bore Cain, saying, "I have gotten a man with the help of the LORD."

Adam knew Eve. What a special word! He knew her the way God had always planned for a husband to know his wife—back when they were naked and not ashamed—one flesh connected, fitted together, and moving together. He knew what it felt like to hug her with no clothes on. *Know* is a word denoting sexual intimacy.

This type of embrace is God's plan for a husband and wife. Consequently, if anyone else, besides a husband and wife, participate in this act it is rebellion against God's plan. This results in more trouble, guilt, and shame in the world. When the couple is not a husband and wife, they are doing things the wrong way—their way instead of God's way.[21] It is ignoring and disobeying God. Knowing each other sexually is sinful between anyone but a married couple.[22]

God also planned something else very special when a husband and wife join together, become one flesh, and know each other this way. Sometimes he chooses to make something happen between their embracing bodies that sends some of the man's special cells, called sperm, into his wife. The sperm can swim up her body tubes and sometimes unite with her special cell called an egg— (a lot like a chicken egg except it stays inside a woman and it doesn't have a hard shell).

God designed the sperm to have coded information about the man and his family in it—color of eyes, hair, and all kinds of things. The

---

[21] God tells us this is wrong and forbids us to practice this in the Ten Commandments. Exodus 20:14.
[22] *The Princess and the Kiss* by Jenny Bishop is a beautifully written and illustrated fairy tale to promote sexual purity in little girls (I know a lot of teens who love the book also.) A princess is given the gift of a kiss and taught to save it for her Prince Charming. I have known mothers who had princess birthday parties and read the book as part of their activities.

egg contains coded information about the wife's body and her family because it was made in her.

When the sperm unites with the woman's egg, (that is the word conceive) God selects some traits from the man and some from the wife and makes a totally different cell. He is creating a baby inside the woman. The baby will be a little like the husband and a little like the wife, but unique and very special.[23] Michael and Steward express and expand this thought in a kid friendly way:

> When a mother elephant and a father elephant join together, they make a baby elephant. But it would be very strange for a mother elephant and a father camel to join together. Actually, they can't.... It would be very distorted—twisted and all mixed up. God has a design for men and women too. A married man and his wife join together and make a baby person.[24] [25]

Genesis 4:1 tells us Adam and Eve had a baby boy named Cain. He probably looked a little like Adam and a little like Eve. He was a gift from God to remind them how much they loved each other and how much God loved them. Babies are always gifts from God (Psalm 127:3).[26]

"God could have made us reproduce the way plants do, with floating spores and pollen. But he preferred human life spring from the

---

[23] Psalm 139 describes how God Himself builds each person in the womb of their mother to be unique and special. Great passage to teach the miracle of conception.

[24] Sally Michael and Gary Steward, *God's Design* (Phillipsburg, New Jersey: P&R Publishing, 2016), 50.

[25] This opens the door for conversation to reinforce the value of life beginning at conception and the amazing design strategy of the Creator: "He made the woman's body to feed and take care of the baby until the baby is born. You can tell the baby is growing inside because the woman's tummy gets bigger and bigger as the baby grows. When the baby gets big enough, she can even move around and kick her mommy when she stretches."

[26] This is a great opportunity to make a personal connection with your child by stating, "You, are my special gift."

exultant, loving embrace of intercourse.[27]" The act of sex is good and acceptable in God's sight because this was His original plan for a husband and wife to know everything about each other and still love and accept each other.

Throughout the Bible, God refers to "oneness" as being linked to a depth of knowledge, and He almost always relates it to the unity of the Trinity (*John* 10:30; *John* 17:4-5). The Trinity always existed, continually expressing the glory of their selfless loving character to one another. The knowledge in this passage (Adam knew Eve) pictures the depth and preciousness of intimacy the Trinity poured out to each other in eternity past that eventually resulted in the birth of creation and man and woman. How awesome that man and woman's sexual knowledge and love produce a child just like the intimacy of the Trinity resulted in birth of mankind!

John Piper masterfully expounds this concept: "God created human beings in his image...and his goal in creating human beings with personhood and passion was to make sure that there would be sexual language and sexual images that would point to the promises and pleasures of God's relationship to his people and our relationship to him. In other words, the ultimate reason (not the only one) why we are sexual is to make God more deeply knowable."[28] He goes on to explain, "God created us with sexual passion so that there would be language to describe what it means to cleave to him in love and what it means to turn away from him to others."[29]

Sex becomes a delight to discuss when we realize that its purpose is to model the spiritual truths that God desires to bestow upon His children, His bride.

---

[27] Bailey. M. *4 Reasons God Supports You Having More Sex With Your Husband.* BeliefNet. https://www.beliefnet.com/love-family/relationships/marriage/4-reasons-god-supports-you-having-more-sex-with-your-husband.aspx.
[28] John Piper and Justin Taylor, *Sex and the Supremacy of Christ* (Wheaton, Illinois: Crossway Books, 2005), 26.
[29] Piper and Taylor, *Sex and the Supremacy of Christ,* 28.

CHAPTER FOUR

A Pathway for Parents

Research shows that the first thing we hear is often taken as truth and establishes a reference point for all future information. The psychology term for this is *Anchoring Bias*. This statement is incredibly frightening and can easily overwhelm us when we think of all that we want our kids to know. There are massive amounts of corrupt agendas seeking to "enlighten" our children for us. We must get the truth to them first before the world introduces enough lies to leave them lost and confused.

As parents, we have a great responsibility to protect our children. Protection comes so easy when we are talking about gun safety, walking across the street, or talking to strangers. We seem to shy away from protecting them emotionally and spiritually. Sex affects all aspects of our being: physical, spiritual, and emotional (Wow, that's how God created us!). This is why it is so important we do everything we can to try to create a healthy desire to follow God's plan for sexual intimacy in marriage by always communicating its sacredness.

Although we do not recommend carelessly rushing out to purchase the most recent social media app to share with your kids, we do want to encourage you to stay current with the culture. This does not necessitate agreeing with the culture. Rather, we should all be intentionally aware of our surroundings in order to cultivate discernment in our children. Our time with them is very short in the grand scheme of life. We need to wisely use this time while we have authority and influence. There will quickly come a time when God intends for us to launch them into the world as arrows (*Psalms* 127:4). We do not want them to break under the pressures of the world. Parents, don't give up. We understand that life is moving faster than ever, and our world is changing so drastically that it is hard to keep up. With the way our world is today, I have often wondered if my kids would even know what truth is. I can be comforted that God's word says, "His truth endures to all generations" (*Psalms* 100:5).

How can we be assured that the information supplied to our children lines up with His truth? That is a great question! The answer lies within His Word and within our homes. We believe that God, in His sovereignty, has laid out a pathway for each of us. This pathway was laid out for us before the foundations of the world (*Ephesians* 1: 3-4). How we choose to walk along this path is left up to us.

It is important to note, we will not be able to fill our children with truth if the truth is not in us. First and foremost, we must be certain in our own standing with Christ before we can ever expect to provide meaningful and lasting instruction as stewards of those placed in our household. I am often reminded of this as I find myself encouraging my daughter. Almost all of the conflicts that occur in our earthy relationships can be cured or resolved by focusing on our identity in Him. Our identity in Christ is foundational and gives the confidence that we need to pursue others and to live out the gospel.

The family unit is the highest earthly calling, second only under marriage between a man and a woman. God has specifically appointed each member. It is helpful to remember He has handpicked each of our children just for us! If we agree that He has appointed every one of our family members, then we can also agree that He has ordained our circle of influence. He has such a sweet plan that allows us to dwell together for our time here on earth. Those with whom we reside, or dwell with, have been gifted to us to join us on this journey called life. Within this sacred institution, we create homes, walls, boundaries, and security. It is within the safe confines of the home that the delicate and essential subject of sexual intimacy should be taught.

God has made it known, throughout scripture, that the home should be a place of worship (*Joshua* 24:15 and *Ephesians* 5). He gave clear instruction to His children to use their homes and their center of influence wisely (*Deuteronomy* 6:5-9). When we speak of His works and teach our children His commandments, we are essentially mapping out the path that God has for them. Sure, we cannot physically take steps for our children, but we should equip them and wisely steer them along. This may also mean redirecting them back to the path if they wander too far. With grace and a lot of patience, we may be granted opportunities to watch God fulfill His promises! Promises that our children need to understand are fulfilled within the boundaries of His path and in the security of Christ.

The House of My Mother

Scripture offers a practical example of a mother who, in her home, successfully trained her child in God's plan for sexual pleasure. The scriptures expounded here are not the ones you will jump into with your child but are intended to motivate you by showing you the end result. It is worth the effort to learn God's intentions for sexual love.

Throughout the *Song of Solomon*, Solomon compliments his bride on her sexual skill. She responds in Chapter Eight by inviting Solomon to take a break from kingdom responsibilities and visit her hometown.

Song of Solomon 8:2a
I would lead you and bring you into the house of my mother—she who used to teach me.

Notice that she credits her mother for teaching her a complete and healthy perspective of both emotional and sexual love.

Song of Solomon 8:2b
I would give you spiced wine to drink, the juice of my pomegranate.

What did her mother teach her? The last part of verse two borrows imagery from the love language Solomon used on their wedding night to passionately communicate how his bride was stimulating him sexually. Her mother had taught her to skillfully intoxicate her future husband with her physical love. These skills are displayed in the lyrics of *Song of Solomon*, Chapter Four which beautifully describes the wedding night. This passage is unpacked in the Epilogue, *Awaken My Love*. It is valuable instruction for your daughter right before her wedding night.

Song of Solomon 8:3
His left hand is under my head, and his right hand embraces me!

The wife describes the memory of how Solomon responded to her love on their wedding night. His arms were wrapped around her, and he was gently fondling her. They both found pleasure on their wedding night because she had been prepared by her mother. Her mother taught her the details of how God designed a man and a woman to stimulate each other sexually. A young lady can trust a God who intentionally planned and teaches such pleasure. What a blessed legacy to pass on to your child!

Song of Solomon 8:4
I adjure you, O daughters of Jerusalem, that you not stir up or awaken love until it pleases.

Verse four is the urgent warning Solomon's wife repeatedly cries out to her virgin girlfriends. I beg you, do not stir up passion and get involved in the progression to sexual love until your wedding night. It is worth waiting for. Do not spoil the precious gift.

Verses six through eight launch into a vivid description of the unquenchable power of true love, then declares the source of this love is the fire flame of Jehovah. How significant to be able to assure a spouse of unending, inextinguishable love all because it is a response to the relentless love of God!

This is a powerful incentive to urge your daughter to passionately pursue a relationship with God so she will be prepared to love her future husband with this abandon. [30]

Solomon's wife continues to explain how her homelife growing up prepared her to be the wife and lover that he so admires. God uses her explanation to provide practical instruction for parents to implement in the home so their children will be directed to purity in future relationships.

Evidently, the wife's father was deceased, so her brothers assisted her mother as guardians. She expounds their philosophy of parenting.

Song of Solomon 8:8-10
We have a little sister, and she has no breasts. What shall we do for our sister on the day when she is spoken for? If she is a wall, we will build on her a battlement of silver, but if she is a door, we will enclose her with boards of cedar. I was a wall, and my breasts were like towers; then I was in his eyes as one who finds peace.

Before she reached puberty, her guardian brothers developed a strategy to use when guys started to show an interest in her. "If she is a wall, impervious to sexual advances from young men, her brothers will adorn her with praise just as a battlement of silver adorns a wall and adds an element of beauty. But if she chooses to be a door—easily entered, easily seduced, the brothers will take a different approach. They will be strict with her, barricading her with planks of cedar in order to protect her virtue."[31] If the young lady was boy crazy, her parents would restrict her. If she was mature and trustworthy, they would reward her.

---

[30] https://subspla.sh/8bf729t is a link to an explanation of these verses. We encourage you to listen to this message with your daughter. Pray before, during, and after. The awe of this love will inspire her to trust her heavenly Father and to anticipate the gift of marital love founded in Him. We worship our God who loves so passionately and whose love can flow through us as the glue that forever seals the beauty of a covenant relationship.

[31] Joseph and Linda Dillow and Peter and Lorraine Pintus, *Intimacy Ignited* (Colorado Springs: Navpress, 20042*)*, 60.

Relax, moms! Because the goal of achieving a deeply emotional and physically satisfying marriage had been openly and explicitly discussed throughout her life, the young Shulamite understood both the urgency for purity and the hope of a blessed sexual future. She very willingly complied with the requests of her guardians, and as an adult, recognized the value of their parenting strategy and was now praising them for their loving care. She explained to Solomon the reason he was so attracted to her, the reason he had eyes for her, was a result of her upbringing. Unlike other self-centered, high maintenance girls, she could be a source of peace and comfort to him. This does not mean the journey will be a piece of cake. Flattery from guys is extremely compelling. Hearing from girlfriends about their escapades with guys can make restrictions seem totally unreasonable and unfair. But the plan is from God. You are not alone. If you are a Christian, you have the Holy Spirit within you to empower you as you hold these conversations with your daughter.

My husband and I never had a girl to train, but I can wholeheartedly say there is nothing that thrills us more than to see our sons treat their wives with respect and to lovingly and unselfishly lead their families with the servant leadership displayed in the life of Christ. To see your married children hug, kiss, hold hands and get excited about romantic get-aways with their spouses brings an indescribable satisfaction. The journey in training them was not easy. As teenagers, they were not always eager to comply with our guidelines, but we persevered in presenting truth the best we knew how at that point in our spiritual walks. If we could redo some of that training, we would spend more time speaking openly, explaining truths and encouraging questions. That's one of the reasons for this book. Hopefully, you will become so enamored with the explanations from God's word that you will confidently present them to your children.

CHAPTER FIVE

Recipe for Romance

We always hear that a girl's wedding night is something she dreams about from the time she is old enough to imagine her Prince Charming. For some of us, it consumes us to the point of no longer just "playing house," but we go as far as to act it out from a very young age. We are influenced by so many voices that tell us what marriage should look like. Sadly, most are ideas that man has created and lie outside of God's divine plan.

When my daughter tried to explain her first crush to me, I questioned how I should respond. It was all so cute and innocent; she did not even know what to call her feelings. She just knew that she was interested in a certain boy who was kind and funny. My husband reminded me that this was natural and that we could use this as an opportunity to talk with her about good qualities to find in a friend (and eventually in a spouse). What we did not do was push for more in the relationship. So many parents encourage "dating" from a dangerously early age (See Appendix A).

As parents, we have tried to be mindful of the love stories our children (specifically our daughter) are exposed to. Hollywood and reality TV certainly do not offer healthy illustrations for her, or us for that matter. We are careful not to ignite feelings and imaginations too early or expose her to media that send her the wrong message of "how to get the guy."

If we want our daughters to value purity, we must continuously and passionately exalt the beauty of creation and the Creator, so that she will view His design for purity as equally lovely. If it seems like a daily battle to defend their purity, that's because it is! Although it isn't 100% fail-proof, I have found that encouraging conversations with my daughter about her views of marriage, as well as allowing her to approach us with any questions, to be remarkably helpful. We have had conversations about impure thoughts, pornography, same-sex attraction, and a vast list of subjects that could threaten her purity. Early on in Chapter 3, I mentioned the great fear that I had about these conversations. I recall cringing and balling up into a fetal position in the bunk bed beneath my daughter as she would unwind from her day. The stories and questions would overwhelm me. Thankfully, she could not see my initial reaction. In those moments God provided grace-filled responses. The Spirit revealed to me that if I wanted her to have hope based on truth and a desire to protect her purity, I needed to fill my responses with beauty and hope, not shame. Since then, I have tried to remind her that she was created with hormones and emotions to help her engage and enjoy her spouse. Our daughters need help to recognize when the enemy attempts to distort God's purposes. Satan wants them to view their emotions and hormones as shameful. This is an opportunity to redirect their thoughts back to God's exciting and glorious plan!

When your daughter is ready, the *Song of Solomon* offers a safe place to see the beauty of God's plan for her precious wedding night! I am forever grateful that God directed me to His Word through the mentoring of Mrs. Debbie. What seemed to have been a plan to destroy me and my daughter has been turned around for His glory! I can now approach these special moments with my daughter with excitement, reverence, and joy. It is okay for her to dream about her future spouse. In fact, it is God-ordained and I pray it will be God-directed.

You may have your own questions like this one: "What is the truth about sex?" There are positive truths as well as negative truths;

both are equally important. If we are not careful, we can focus too heavily on the consequences of the misuse of sex out of fear and a genuine desire to protect. When we think about sexual instruction for our children, we tend to overload the conversation with warnings. Warnings are necessary; but first of all, we need to direct them to a path of benefits so they will deeply desire God's best. Whenever discernment causes us to withhold information for a time, may we encourage them to trust God with the unknowns until His timing is right.

"If we talk only of what is off limits, we miss what is good."[32] So what good message do we need to convey? God powerfully provides the recipe for romance in the *Song of Solomon*. Parents, don't forget God's message is for you too. A healthy marriage, modeled for our children, is a priceless guide.

Ingredients for Romance

Why use the *Song of Solomon*? Duguid says, "The Song paints a glorious picture of the marriage relationship between a man and a woman that is so rich and deep that we should all long to have a relationship just like that."[33] With its vivid descriptions, *The Song* illustrates the freedom and depth of physical pleasure God designed. This builds trust in God's plan for sexual intimacy (to be experienced within a married union between husband and wife). Girls who embrace this picture will want the same blessed romance and will likely have more motivation to pursue relationships God's way.

Song of Solomon 1:1
The Song of Songs, which is Solomon's.

---

[32] Charles, Tyler, "Why 'Don't Do It' Doesn't Work," https://www.christianitytoday.com/pastors/2015/spring/why-dont-do-it-doesnt-work.html
[33] Ian M. Duguid, *Song of Songs: An Introduction and Commentary* (Phillipsburg, NJ: P&R Publishing, 2016), 9.

God is declaring that this book is the most beautiful and powerful love song ever written. It is the song of all songs.[34] Not only does *The Song*[35] describe the beauty and freedom of love between a husband and wife, but it also represents the caring, selfless love that Christ has for His bride. Like most songs, it is poetry. Throughout the song, the groom (Solomon) refers to his bride (Shulamite) as *my love*. The bride addresses the groom as *my beloved.* These phrases clue us in on who is speaking.

Most commentators agree *The Song* begins on the wedding day with random thoughts of the bride to be.

Song of Solomon 1:2
Let him kiss me with the kisses of his mouth! For your love is better than wine;

Like every bride before her wedding, Shulamite is daydreaming of her first night with her groom. She looks forward to privacy and kissing. The word used for love is *dodem*—which is an intimately physical or sexual love that speaks of kisses and caresses.[36] Shulamite anticipates the sheer pleasure of merging with her husband to be more intoxicating than wine.

Song of Solomon 1:3
Your anointing oils are fragrant; your name is oil poured out; therefore virgins love you.

The bride recalls how the scent of Solomon's anointing oils are so fragrant they cause her to want to draw close. Whenever we hold a baby that has just had a bath, the fragrance of the shampoo and baby wash make him even more cuddly. We experience a compulsion to hug

---

[34] The literary form of the book is a lyric idyll. It is a song that tells a story, similar to a movie with flash backs. Its interpretation can vary but the overall general purpose and message can be reasoned out.
[35] From this point forward in the text, the authors may choose to refer to *The Song of Solomon* as *The Song*.
[36] Joseph Dillow, *Solomon on Sex* (Nashville, TN: Thomas Nelson, Inc), 13.

that baby close and kiss him all over his face, his head, and even those chubby little toes. That's exactly how the bride is dreaming of her groom. Her man smells so good, she desires to snuggle up and lay kisses all over him.

The best thing about this scene is that it is not a girl in a chick flick fantasizing about being swallowed up in their lover's arms. This description is coming from The Word of God, and He has declared this is the song of all songs—the most beautiful that has ever been written. A God that would applaud sexual intimacy in this way is a God whom singles can trust with their future love life. This is His exhilarating plan and design.

As previously noted, wedding day thoughts often vacillate all over the place. The thought of expensive perfume launches the young bride to consider its exceptional value. Then the thought leads her to express gratitude and thanks for the *name* of her husband. It is not just that his name has the benefits of royalty; but in scripture, name represents the character of a person. Like flowers and spices that have been pressed into fragrant oil, his character has been tested by the stress of life and has emerged as priceless treasure. She has utmost respect for him. God is alerting singles to the importance of good character in a prospective mate and in a successful future sex life.

The bride is confident in their sexual relationship because she is able to confirm her groom's integrity and character. She can freely give herself to him because she respects him and knows his character is exceptional.

Moms, now is the time to dialogue about recognizing respectable character in a future mate (See Appendix A). What is important and what does it look like? Why is character consideration important for one's future sexual life?

For starters, a prospective mate must be a Christian. 2 Corinthians 6:14[37] strongly warns Christians not to enter covenant with unbelievers. If your child is a believer, the most important aspect of her life and being should be Christ. Decisions, purpose and happiness

---

[37] *Do not be unequally yoked with unbelievers. For what partnership has righteousness with lawlessness? Or what fellowship has light with darkness?*

should all revolve around Him. Marriage partners should share every aspect of life. If she wants to walk hand in hand and heart to heart with her mate, they need to powerfully connect around what is most important to her —Jesus Christ. They need to be looking at the same "horizon." A mate who is not a believer does not have the capacity to become one spiritually with a believer. Our Loving Father is not limiting our relationships with this directive; He is directing us to the best relationship.

Why emphasize observing character before a couple is involved in a relationship? Because once a couple enters a relationship, they become infatuated and lose all objectivity (See Appendix A for additional character considerations).

Notice in verse three that all the virgins love Solomon. Shulamite's friends confirm that he is respectable, a man of integrity whom they can easily admire. God is emphasizing that people who care about us should be able to recognize quality character traits in our prospective mate and should speak into our lives with either approval or disapproval. Ryken says, "She will only pursue this relationship with the support of her faith community. She wants the people around her—especially godly women—to bless and celebrate this relationship, which is not exclusively private but inclusively public."[38]

Song of Solomon 1:4
Draw me after you; let us run.

"Draw me" means to lead me. "Let us run" seems to say, let's do life together. Shulamite is so confident in Solomon's character that she is ready to follow his lead. She can trust him.

This is significant. Not only does this verse acknowledge that Solomon possesses admirable leadership skills, but the bride is acknowledging her willingness to biblically submit to her husband's leadership. This principle is foundational for a Christian marriage. Young women desperately need a biblical understanding of a

---

[38] Philip Ryken, *Love of Loves in the Song of Songs,* (Wheaton, Illinois: Crossway, 2019), 35.

husband's leadership and a wife's submission so they, like this bride, can determine if they are willing to commit to forever live out life with their fiancé . Conversations with your daughter are so much more than a plan to avoid inappropriate physical intimacy—but preparation for marriage itself (See Appendix C).

Song of Solomon 1:4b
The king has brought me into his chambers.

Reality hits. This new life is about to begin. She is in the palace.

Song of Solomon 1:4c
We will exult and rejoice in you; we will extol your love more than wine; rightly do they love you.

The chorus, the daughters of Jerusalem (the other virgins of the land),[39] burst into song to voice their agreement that they celebrate the character of Solomon. They admire both the relationship and the love Solomon shows his bride-to-be. The bride immediately reinforces their admiration of her husband-to-be.

Continually remind your daughter that Solomon and every godly husband picture the love of Christ for His bride. The selfless covenant love of Christ calls for celebration. Finding a husband who embraces this type of love also calls for an expression of gratitude and joy.

Song of Solomon 1:5-6
I am very dark, but lovely, O daughters of Jerusalem, like the tents of Kedar, like the curtains of Solomon. Do not gaze at me because I am dark, because the sun has looked upon me. My mother's sons were angry with me; they made me keeper of the vineyards, but my own vineyard I have not kept!

---

[39] Another feature of this lyric idyll is the imaginary chorus referred to as the daughters of Jerusalem. The chorus is used to offer words of advice and signal transition to a different scene.

Background is needed here. The bride grew up in Lebanon where her brothers (mother's sons) who were her guardians, made a living by working in the family vineyards. She complains that her strict brothers made her work in the vineyards where she acquired a suntan and developed muscles. As a result, she did not have the luxury of pampering her complexion (her own vineyard).

The cultural standard for beauty during Solomon's time is soft, fair skin. When Shulamite looks around the palace at the dignified, elegant daughters of Jerusalem, she must feel a bit intimidated because her muscular dark appearance is so different than the standard.

Females tend to be obsessive about looks. Let's face it. We all feel like we are fat, and we fret over every blemish and frizz. This can quickly get annoying, especially to males. Moms can prepare their daughters by teaching them that a man can be stimulated and satisfied even when our features and looks may not be as striking as the cover of a magazine (See Appendix A). Solomon's bride offers a great example of how to combat concerns over looks.

She asks the daughters of Jerusalem not to judge her, then gives examples of dark yet deeply admired artifacts. The tents of Kedar were constructed from black goat's hair that was known to sparkle in the sun, and the expensive tapestries hanging in the palace were woven with rich dark colors of wool.[40] Rather than obsess over her inadequacies, Solomon's fiancé chose to think on the positive aspects of what she has to offer her husband and then concentrate on pleasing him. So, Shulamite shifts her attention to her groom.

Song of Solomon 1:7
Tell me, you whom my soul loves, where you pasture your flock, where you make it lie down at noon; for why should I be like one who veils herself beside the flocks of your companions?

Joseph Dillow suggests that since the bride is a country girl, used to rural living, her mind naturally pictures Solomon, the king, as the

---

[40] Joseph Dillow, *Solomon on Sex* (Nashville: Thomas Nelson, 1977), 14.

shepherd of the flock of Israel.[41] She questions what his career will look like once they are married. She voices concern that the demands of his responsibilities will require him to be gone frequently and will unreasonably limit their time together. Will she be able to handle this lifestyle? Will she be so lonely that she will be tempted to wander out in search for him?

"One who veils herself" is a reference to the dress and behavior of a prostitute. If Shulamite leaves the palace to hunt for her husband, she may appear to be a woman who chases guys. His companions may get the wrong impression of her.

Joseph Dillow expounds the young lady's thought pattern:

> She gently warns Solomon that if she has to go out searching for him, she will violate local propriety and might encourage overtures from other men including some of his companions. The very thought of appearing immodest or of encouraging the affections of other men is morally repulsive to her. She loves only one man and does not want to even suggest she could have an interest in another.[42]

This verse provides a great opportunity to open dialogue with your daughter about appropriate dress and behavior.[43] Females are often labeled by their looks and conduct, especially their dress. Girls who purposefully position themselves where they know a guy will be coming out of class, attending an event, or hanging out can give the impression that they are stalking guys. Girls who entice the one she has her eyes on by exposing too much skin or with the wiggle in their walk will end up with a partner who is more interested in what he can get than who she is as a person (*Proverbs* 7:10-12). "Being out and about,

---

[41] Dillow, *Solomon on Sex*, 15.
[42] Dillow, *Solomon on Sex*, 16.
[43] I highly recommend Mary Kassion's book, *Girls Gone Wise in a World Gone Wild*. The author very skillfully expounds scriptures comparing God's plan for godly women vs. women of irreputable behavior. Girls are taught to engage the culture without embracing it.

dangling your body as bait, and lying in wait to hook a man isn't just bad for the man who walks into your trap; it's also bad for you!...You won't find the long-term, loving relationship you yearn for."[44]

Song of Solomon 1:8
If you do not know, O most beautiful among women, follow in the tracks of the flock, and pasture your young goats beside the shepherds' tents.

Solomon responds in verse eight by relieving her insecurities. First, he praises her for her beauty. He finds her attractive, regardless of the cultural standard of beauty. That's the kind of fiancé you desire for your child. Next, he picks up on her shepherd imagery and explains that he will leave tracks (an itinerary) for her so that she can directly join him instead of wandering aimlessly in search of him.

Song of Solomon 1:9
I compare you, my love, to a mare among Pharaoh's chariots.

Solomon continues to reassure his new bride that she is the one he finds attractive. He addresses her as "my love" or "my darling." She is his lifelong companion. Then, he compares her to a mare among Pharaoh's chariots. How insulting! No, not in Solomon's world. Solomon loved horses and owned thousands of very expensive ones. They were prized possessions to him and to the middle eastern culture.

When we toured the Kentucky Horse Museum, we found several plaques with quotes or statements about Arabian mares:

> Take upon you the mares! Their backs are a sanctuary
> and their wombs are a treasure.
>
> Muhammad

---

[44] Kassian, *Girls Gone Wise in a World Gone Wild*, 86.

> The three most precious possessions are a mare, followed by her daughter in foal with a filly.
>
> Old Arab Saying

> A good quality "asil" mare was the most prestigious possession a man could have and her purity was strenuously protected.
>
> Legendary Practices of Arabian Horse Breeding

Solomon was declaring that his bride was the most cherished possession he had. But to add that the mare was among Pharaoh's chariots greatly intensified the value. The footnotes in my Bible explain:

> Pharaoh's chariots with their twin stallions would be well-known and much admired in Israel. What is envisaged here would have been exceptional, a bejeweled mare among the stallions, causing wonder and excitement.[45]

Solomon conveys that the beauty and elegance of his bride is so exceptional that he feels like a trained stallion in Pharaoh's chariots that has been hitched with a stunning mare. He is so distracted by her beauty that he cannot concentrate. She drives him wild.

What a way with words! Solomon is a master at romantic communication. What girl would not feel loved?

Song of Solomon 1:10-11
Your cheeks are lovely with ornaments, your neck with strings of jewels. We will make for you ornaments of gold, studded with silver. While the king was on his couch, my nard gave forth its fragrance. My beloved is to me a sachet of myrrh that lies between my breasts. My beloved is to me a cluster of henna blossoms in the vineyards of Engedi.

---

[45] The Reformation Study Bible (Lake Mary, FL: Ligonier Ministries, 2005), 938.

He acknowledges the details of her attire. He not only approves the accessories she is wearing (probably gifts from him) but promises future gifts of more jewelry.

The conversation becomes a dialogue of admiration as the bride responds by highlighting the character of Solomon in verses 12-14. The king is sitting on his couch across from her. She references nard and myrrh, both expensive, prized fragrances. The custom was to gather a signature mixture of spices, blossoms, and oils into a packet to wear like a necklace at night. Hence the packet between her breasts. The fragrances would permeate the skin all night. Then the next day the delicate signature fragrance would gently emit from the skin identifying the wearer as she walked by. This is a metaphor for the way the bride envisions Solomon lying between her breasts, bringing out the best in her. She expresses utmost admiration for him by inferring she is a better person when she is with him. What a valuable trait for a spouse!

The bride also compares her groom to henna blossoms, a fragrant desert flower commonly found in the foliage of an oasis. When life is dry, filled with waste, she finds her groom to be refreshing. He lifts her spirits. This is the reason she wants to grow old with him. This is the type of guy you want your daughter to marry.

The bride found her groom attractive because when she was around him, she was a better person. He brought out the best in her. One of our nieces was dating a young man from her church. His dad was a deacon; his mom was actively involved in the church, so our niece's parents had readily approved of the relationship. But they started to notice that their daughter's attitude had gradually changed. She had become increasingly negative and cynical. The parents realized the young man was hyper-critical of the world around him, and his influence upon their daughter caused her to view her world differently. This was a toxic relationship—opposite of the positive relationship Shulamite had experienced with Solomon.

We want our daughters to live forever with someone who is so attuned to the love and character of our God that he will redeem her thought life with reverence and hope that comes only from a close walk with Jesus. Shulamite recognized this in Solomon. Our children can recognize this trait if throughout their lives, we offer praise for individuals who possess this influence.

Solomon 1:15
Behold, you are beautiful, my love; behold, you are beautiful; your eyes are doves.

Solomon gives his bride his full attention. He cannot get over how delightful she is and loves to repeatedly voice this to her. The eyes of a dove are peaceful and because doves often represent purity, Solomon could be complimenting her virginity. It is the wedding night, and she has never known a man sexually. Solomon finds this appealing, so appealing that he specifically compliments her.

Turtle doves, also referenced by Solomon in Chapter Two, are known to mate for life.[46] Solomon could be cherishing the expectation that his new wife will remain faithful to him for life.

Titus Chapter 2 challenges older women to train younger women to exercise *philandrous or* "husband love" in their marriage (Highest on the priority list of young women to train are our daughters). In her explanation of this principle, Mary Farrar says,

> God has called us to fix our hearts upon our husbands in a special "one-man-kind-of-woman" love. Philandrous means that we prefer him over all others, that we accept him simply as he is, that we understand and value his manhood, that we seek to meet his unique needs as a man living in a post flood world, that we regard our husband and treat him with respect, and that we express our feelings of affection to him.[47]

My college roommate's fiancé had a friend from Pakistan. This friend was not only receiving a quality education in the states, but he was greatly enjoying what he called "fast" American women. He

---

[46] http://bioweb.uwlax.edu/bio203/s2009/schreine_sara/reproduction.htm
[47] Mary Farrar, *Choices* (Sisters, Oregon: Multnomah Books, 1994), 181.

enjoyed partying and sexual encounters with the girls he met. Since he had no obligation to these girls, he could quickly move on to other girls. What a provocative lifestyle he had discovered!

Surprisingly, he was very quick to explain to his roommate that when he got ready to settle down to marry, he would return to Pakistan to find a virgin who was a "one-man-kind-of-woman" who would be faithful to him. Solomon was intimating approval that his bride was a "one-man-kind-of-woman."

When I was in college, one of my summer jobs was working at a car wash. I directed cars onto the track that pulled them through the brushes, then dried the cars, cleaned windows, vacuumed, and wiped interiors. I had a partner who performed the tasks on one side of the car while I cleaned the opposite side. Although our personalities were different, we were good friends and made an efficient team. She was stunningly beautiful and witty. Our supervisor was a few years older, recently divorced, and found significance in impressing young coeds. On slower days, he would come sit and chat with us. Once he made the comment that my partner was the kind of girl he would like to date, but that I was the kind of girl he would want to marry. I never let on to either of them, but I was deeply hurt. I felt like he was saying that my partner was fun to be with, and I, on the other hand, would make a dependable, conscientious housekeeper. Thankfully, my team member could see through him and was not at all seduced by his flirting. I realize now that being a "one-man-kind-of-woman" (someone who reserves herself for the man she plans to love all her life) is indeed the type of faithful wife that I want to be. Solomon and the Lord see this trait as honorable.

The next verses through *Song of Solomon* 2:7 uncover the preciousness of purity and faithfulness. The picture is sweet and powerful. I pray that the heart of these truths will capture your daughter and create a longing within her to move towards becoming a "one-man-kind-of-woman."

Recipe for Romance

Solomon 1:16-17

Behold, you are beautiful, my beloved, truly delightful. Our couch is green; the beams of our house are cedar; our rafters are pine.

Shulamite deeply desires to live up to the description Solomon has just admired. She sincerely declares that her beloved is a handsome man. She is delighted that his heart belongs to her.

She shifts attention to the bridal chamber he has prepared for her. Traditionally, a groom would spend the year before the actual wedding day preparing a home for his bride to be. Often extended families lived together so the prospective groom would construct a special bedroom, attached to his father's house, for him and his bride after their wedding. He normally took great pains to furnish it as beautifully as he could. Because his bride would be leaving her native country and familiar surroundings, Solomon, in an attempt to defray the pain of homesickness, very thoughtfully designed a bridal chamber from fir and cedar. Lebanon, where Shulamite grew up, was known for its fir and cedar. The room smelled and looked like home to her. Even the canopied bed was green to remind her of the outdoors. How sweet of him!

When her groom gifted her with such precious consideration, she immediately expressed gratitude. Notice, that throughout their day, before the wedding ceremony, during the wedding feast, and now as they enter their bedroom the couple repeatedly exchange admiration, reassurance, and expressions of devotion. This is the way God designed that a couple approach physical intimacy, by touching hearts before touching bodies.

Linda Dillow says that the mind is the most important sexual organ.[48] Thinking and conveying positive, admirable thoughts is the first essential step to romance. Throughout life, training your daughter to take note of the kindness and character of others will prepare her to recognize the character traits in a Christlike husband. This will also train her to quickly and sincerely express gratitude for the little acts of

---

[48] Linda Dillow and Lorraine Pintus, *Intimate Issues* (Colorado Springs, Colorado: Waterbrook Press, 1999), 23.

kindness her future husband showers on her. This will forever strengthen and develop the husband-wife bond. Remember you are not just protecting her purity but preparing her for a fulfilling marriage.

Notice in these verses that the bedroom was a haven—an escape from the stresses of life. The people from bible times would hang luxurious linen on their walls, powder their sheets and burn incense to create a relaxing, but loving atmosphere.

When my four sons were young, I was concerned that I keep the family room and kitchen somewhat presentable in case someone stopped by. My washing machine never stopped in those days, so I would stash all those baskets of unfolded laundry out of sight in my bedroom. I was also helping Sam with a business venture. I would stack the mail, bookkeeping, and orders on my dresser until I had time to process through them. That "time" was very slow to appear in my schedule so our bedroom was a jumble of what I could not get done—certainly not an escape from stress. One day after Sam studied verses 15 and 16, he came home and instructed me to pick out fresh paint and a matching bedspread and pillows for our bed. He explained to me how we were going to transform our bedroom to our retreat center. I realized my husband and our relationship were more important than any visitor that might come by; so to this day, I consider our bedroom the most important room in our home.

I cannot help but be reminded that our Heavenly Bridegroom is preparing a luxurious place of retreat for us, an everlasting get away, free from the stress and burden of sin. Remind your daughter that when she and her future husband make the effort to create an inviting bedroom atmosphere, aesthetically and emotionally, they will not just be mimicking HGTV, but shadowing their future home in glory. Every aspect of their future marriage should picture the relationship of Christ and **His bride.**

CHAPTER SIX

Private Property
Protected Area

Protection is often issued or announced on Warning or Notice signs. These signs are generally posted to benefit the one seeking pleasure, rather than to deprive them. These warnings can be interpreted differently based on the heart of the receiver. The receiver has a choice — will they recognize the intention of the one with authority and choose to respectfully obey for their safety, or will they rebel and choose to rely on their own understanding?

When God gave Adam and Eve a warning notice, the enemy quickly invaded Eve's thoughts with his spin on the warning, "You will not surely die."[49] "If God really loves you, why would He withhold His wonderful gifts?"

Eve was easily deceived into questioning God's character. In similar fashion, we can be tricked into believing that we are missing out on something to be desired.

Truly, God loves us so much that He offers protection of His glorious gifts. He even provides instructions for how to enjoy them to the fullest capacity! I needed to find a way to adequately express this

---

[49] *Genesis* 3:4

loving character of God to my daughter. Milton Vincent provides a beautiful explanation in *A Gospel Primer*. "The gospel changes my view of God's commandments; in that it helps me to see the heart of the Person from whom those commandments come."[50] He goes on further to remind us that we can see them as, "friendly signposts from a heavenly Father who is seeking to love me through each directive, so that I might experience His very fullness forever."[51]

One of the best ways for us to communicate the benefits of these "protected areas" to our children is with joy and excitement. Rather than just attempting to establish hard boundaries that they cannot cross, we can passionately describe the beauty of what lies inside of God's path. We get the privilege of building anticipation in their hearts. It is essential to also explain the perils that are present. The enemy strategizes to distract and encourage rebellion against God. He knows it is in our very nature to seek our own way. He also knows the weakness of our flesh when sexual desires are ignited. He is fully aware of the beauty of God's creation and plan for sex and is, therefore, plotting in any way he can to destroy it.

"In the same way (as dynamite), the desires that men and women have to love and enjoy each other are powerful and good; and, yet, they can be harmful and destructive if they are not handled with care and used as God designed them."[52] Sex is not something we should completely avoid because of its potentially dangerous nature, but rather something we should treat with incredible respect. Voltaire, a French Enlightenment writer, stated: "With great power comes great responsibility." This principle is better illustrated in *Luke* 12:48, "Everyone to whom much was given, of him much will be required." Sex is such a wonderful gift that if pursued off God's path (outside of marriage), it becomes an imminent danger to us and no longer enjoyable as God intended. When sinful man attempts to trespass and experience sex outside of the guidelines that God has given us, we step outside of His protection.

---

[50] Milton Vincent, *A Gospel Primer for Christians* (Bemidji, MN: Focus Publishing, 2008), 18.
[51] Vincent, *A Gospel Primer for Christians,* 18.
[52] Michael, and Steward, *God's Design,* 82.

Private Property

Recently, my kids discovered an old song that they enjoy singing. The music is uplifting and the chorus is catchy. So much so, that my husband and I found ourselves jumping right in with them as we were blaring the song along our short ride to church one evening. I began to sing the cute chorus the next morning as I encouraged my kids to "Come and Get Their Love"[53] in the form of hugs before they rushed off to school. It seemed harmless — until I read the full lyrics. Lines like, "Cause you're fine, and you're mine, and you look so divine" and, "Go on and love it if you like it...It's your business if you want some, take some," caught me by surprise. It may have been released in 1973, but this is still how Satan persuades our culture to view sex today. "If you desire it, go ahead and take it. You deserve it."

It is paramount that our daughters understand the dangers of this notion. It is equally as critical that we present a proper understanding of our Creator's grand design! Prepare her for the precious gift, wrapped and sealed with love by our Heavenly Father, to be received on her wedding day!

Don't Awaken Love

God initiates the wonder of experiencing the gift by emphasizing the vital importance of positive, loving communication between a husband and wife who are approaching the act of love. In this song, the communication began early in the day as the couple attended the wedding feast with their guests (*Song of Solomon* 1). Now in Chapter Two of the *Song*, the praise and sincere comments continue to be exchanged in the bridal chamber:

Song of Solomon 2:1
I am a rose of Sharon, a lily of the valleys.

---

[53] Redbone. "Come and Get Your Love." *Wovoka.* Lolly and Pat Vegas. 1973.

Thoughts of all the bride has experienced and seen crowd her mind, and the insecurity about her appearance begins to surface again. The ladies in the palace are noticeably refined and elegant. This country girl describes herself as a rose of Sharon and a lily of the valley. These are common wildflowers along the Mediterranean coast lands. She feels like a dandelion in the middle of a bouquet of exquisite roses. But notice how sensitively Solomon responds to her insecurities.

Song of Solomon 2:2
As a lily among brambles, so is my love among the young women.

Solomon romantically and skillfully calms her inhibitions by turning her metaphor around, "You are a lily alright, a lily in the middle of a field of thorns."

Song of Solomon 2:3
As an apple tree among the trees of the forest, so is my beloved among the young men. With great delight I sat in his shadow, and his fruit was sweet to my taste.

His sweet assurance frees her to forget her insecurities and, instead, ponder his handsome features. She accelerates the conversation to a sexual level when she compares him to an apple tree among the trees of the forest. Apples were thought to be aphrodisiacs that stimulated sexual desire. His physique is appealing to her. Now at last, they are alone, and she lets him know she is anticipating sexual union with him.

This bride is delighted that her husband is drawn close and is on top of her (casting a shadow). The language indicates they are kissing, and she finds the moment as pleasurable as she imagined in Chapter One.

Song of Solomon 2:4
He brought me to the banqueting house, and his banner over me was love.

Private Property

Shulamite enlightens Solomon to another reason the thought of sexual love is so appealing to her. When he brought her to the banqueting house for the wedding feast, his banner over her was love. Banners were flags used for identification. To be under the banner means a person belongs to what the banner is representing. The flag infers a sense of strength and protection. The word used for love (*ahabah*) can have a sexual connotation but, at the same time, conveys a strong sense of covenant, of a commitment to love and protect the way the Lord covenants to always do what is best for His bride.[54] The things Solomon said to his bride, the reassurance and promises he made to her when they were at the feast (in our last chapter), gave her a sense of belonging and security. Wives long for security to know they are cherished and cared for.

The love he displayed through his reassuring words were the basis and confidence for her pursuit of sexual love. She feels liberated to freely love him. The language used here could have double meaning. She is at the true banqueting house now where she can at last, away from the guests, feast on his physical love.

Song of Solomon 2:5
Sustain me with raisins; refresh me with apples, for I am sick with love.

The intensity of this sexual desire escalates so rapidly she feels weak and asks him to sustain her with raisins and apples. This fruit was thought to be an aphrodisiac or a stimulant to arouse sexual desire. She is essentially saying her passion is building, and she wants him to continue to stimulate her. The bride describes the way Solomon complies with her request:

Song of Solomon 2:6
His left hand is under my head, and his right hand embraces me!

His arms are wrapped around her. His left hand is under her head, probably directing her gaze to fasten on his eyes. His right hand

---

[54]Dillow and Pintus, *Intimacy Ignited*, 70.

is holding her. The word, to embrace (*habaq*), carries the connotation, "to fondle." He is gently stroking her body with sexual touch.

The arousal described here teaches a progression from kind compliments and loving conversation early in the day to conversation expressing sexual attraction and anticipation. The progression advances to kisses and gentle touch, then more passionate kissing and fondling.

I marvel that our Father, in His Living Word, lays out a plan of step-by-step stimulation for a wife's body so that she can experience maximum pleasure from this sacred uniting act. A female's body, just like her mind, is complicated. While a man is very quickly stimulated visually, a female's body requires gentle stimulation to be prepared to receive her husband's love organ into her love chamber.

God's intention is that the dialogue, the sexual comments, the gentle kissing with nonsexual touch, then the passionate kissing with fondling be a beautiful flow that climaxes into the actual physical act of love. Chapter Four and Chapter Seven prove God's intent that a married couple experience both emotional and sexual fulfillment by describing the progression in even more vivid detail (See Epilogue).

We pray the power and beauty that is in this passage will generate an awe in your daughter's heart so she will trust God and His ways implicitly by reserving herself for her wedding night.

Song of Solomon 2:1-6 entrances us as God tenderly outlines the passionate progression leading to the act of sexual intercourse. Then very abruptly, the song shifts gears when Shulamite interrupts her recollection of this precious scene.

Song of Solomon 2:7
I adjure you, O daughters of Jerusalem, by the gazelles or the does of the field, that you not stir up or awaken love until it pleases.

As this bride sings the glorious memory of her wedding night, she is begging her girlfriends, the daughters of Jerusalem, the virgins of the land to heed her urgent warning. Gazelles and does are both graceful deerlike creatures, known for their sexual playfulness. Shulamite pleads for the sake of this precious, sacred, stimulating love, do not get involved in this progression—do not stir up, do not awaken this love until the time is right. The right time is your wedding night. This is worth waiting for. God is not keeping singles from sex; He is saving them for sex.

Singles hear plenty of warnings that insist they wait until their wedding night to make love, but this warning from our Creator is much more specific than "Don't go all the Way." He actually instructs singles to avoid the progression leading to the sexual act.

Why would He warn against the progression, against stirring up love, against awakening love? Paul explains to the Thessalonians that sex is holy and sacred to God.

1 Thessalonians 4:3-8
For this is the will of God, your sanctification: that you abstain from sexual immorality; that each one of you know how to control his own body in holiness and honor, not in the passion of lust like the Gentiles who do not know God; that no one transgress and wrong his brother in this matter, because the Lord is an avenger in all these things, as we told you beforehand and solemnly warned you. For God has not called us for impurity, but in holiness. Therefore, whoever disregards this, disregards not man but God who gives His Holy Spirit to you.

Paul warns all Christians to refrain from or stay away from sexual sin. The act of intercourse is sacred and holy. It represents the picture of our Savior who surrendered His body and entire being for His bride, the church. Paul exhorts all humans to know how to control their body so no one will violate the sacredness of God's plan or violate another human life. Allowing lust and sexual passion to control body behavior before marriage is rebellion against the sacredness of God's plan. It is transgressing (crossing the line into the culturally accepted, but ungodly behavior of unbelievers). Paul declares each person needs the knowledge, skill, and desire to master his/her own body so that, out of reverence for God, that body will function in holiness.

Singles tend to push the envelope by asking, "Where is the line?" The Thessalonian passage shows the line is the passion of lust or any speech, touch, or action that stirs lustful thoughts or desires. Lust is an uncontrolled desire to have and possess what is not rightfully ours. In other words, it is often a God-given desire that is out of control. The progression God described in the first six verses of *Song of Solomon* Chapter Two and, later, in more explicit detail in Chapters Four and Seven were divinely designed to stimulate strong desire for your marriage partner (See Epilogue). The Shulamite acknowledges the power of the progression to drive a couple into a consuming union. As the body naturally responds to this strong drive, it does not stop to see if wedding rings are on fingers. It just performs the way the Master Designer planned. This is why Solomon's bride pleads with the virgins of the land, her girlfriends, not to stir up or awaken this love. Acting on the desire to sexually embrace, fondle, and unite with another body before entering a covenant of marriage blasphemes the sacredness of the marriage union. Christ did not give His body for unbelievers or those who are not in covenant with Him. His relationship is limited to His bride. Our relationships are to be patterned after His. We give our bodies solely to the one with whom we enter the covenant of marriage.

The Shulamite recognizes the sacredness of the gift of sex and warns her girlfriends not to get involved in the progression because the passion fueled by the progression is intended by God to powerfully drive the body into the sexual act. Many Christian couples emotionally enter the progression during a dating relationship. Their intention is to call a stop to their behavior before they rip their clothes off. The feeling is that they have not violated God's instructions because they have not "gone all the way." The problem is, God did not design bodies to halt. His intention is that the passion be a flow that intensifies into a surge of emotional and physical expression. If an unmarried couple repeatedly enters the progression, and repeatedly restrains the body, eventually the God-given bodily dynamics will prevail, resulting in the couple's finding themselves in the act of intercourse.

Reasons to avoid progression before the wedding night:

1) In order to reverently represent Him, God warns to reserve this sacred act for marriage. The progression generates lust (over desire). Following the bodily progression outside of marriage degrades the holiness of God. His word is filled with warnings.[55]
2) The female body is designed to follow God's plan of uninterrupted passion. The progression is God's way of preparing her body to receive her husband's love. Repeatedly halting the progression before a couple goes all the way trains the female body to shut down. Once married, when the couple can rightfully enjoy sexual union, the female body shuts down and has trouble achieving orgasm. She often becomes frigid.
3) Males will view the progression as "what you do while dating." Since their bodies require only minimal stimulation, once husbands are married, they will be eager to quickly proceed straight to the act of love and tend to minimize the foreplay which is necessary to lubricate and prepare the female body for fulfillment. A wife will experience the pain of an unprepared body and the despair of feeling like nothing more than a sexual object for her husband's pleasure.
4) Because God's design is so potent, most couples will find themselves unable to repeatedly restrain what God designed to progress. The results often include guilt, unwed pregnancy, date rape, or contraction of an STD.

You may be thinking the description of the progression was a product of years of Hallmark sentimentality where we are just fitting those romantic thoughts to scripture. But scientific research into the function of our hormones and our reproductive system points to a Creative Designer who insured the progression would be part of our life experience. A team of scientists from Rutgers University[56] determined

---

[55] Flee Fornication (1 *Corinthians* 6:18); Warning to young men (Proverbs 5).
[56] Helen Fisher, *Lust, Attraction, and Attachment in Mammalian Reproduction* in *Human Nature. Vol 9. No. 1,* (New York: Medical Journal, 1988), 23-52.

that love can be broken into the categories of lust, attraction, and attachment. These three categories are based on the release of hormones from the hypothalamus when our brain recognizes we are entering each phase.[57] We were created in such an amazing way that our body not only recognizes that we are developing an attraction to someone (by releasing testosterone, estrogen, dopamine, norepinephrine, and serotonin), but ultimately rewards us with good feelings (oxytocin and vasopressin) and lasting attachment. Oxytocin has been referred to as the "love hormone." This hormone is released during non-romantic interactions that are intimate in nature, like parent-child bonding, touch/hug, and such. We all need the proper amounts of these hormones to thrive. However, too much of these same hormones can lead to addiction. Our bodies are wired in a way that can allow us to become "Hooked on a Feeling."[58] Remember the steps of the progression. The emotional connection of positive communication progresses to gentle kisses and soft touch, which releases hormones that intentionally stir an addiction for more. The scientists had no idea the phases had been laid out in verses 1-6 of the *Song of Songs*. Every love song ever written recognizes and highlights the phases and urges us to pursue the good feelings produced by the hormones.

Once again, we see that God's plan is perfect, and His design of our bodies and sex are without flaw. When we advance from non-sexual to sexual touch, our bodies are created to respond as if we are becoming "one flesh" as God intended in marriage. The hypothalamus does not know if we are not married. Hormones are released and bonds are made. I once heard it explained as though you are becoming cemented together with the one in which you choose to become sexually involved. If this is not your spouse and the relationship ends, you will be forced through much pain to sever the bond that God intended to forever represent His perfect unending love.

---

[57](2017) SITNBoston "Love, Actually: The science behind lust, attraction, and companionship. https://sitn.hms.harvard.edu/flash/2017/love-actually-science-behind-lust-attraction-companionship/
[58] Thomas, B.J. "Hooked on a Feeling". Chips Moman. Scepter Music Inc. 1968

Private Property

How great the Father's love for us! He not only designed the passion and pleasure of sex as an exclusive bonding mechanism for husband and wife to represent the commitment Christ has for His bride, the church, but He discloses the path to follow to reach that glorious haven and gives us hormones to ensure we reach that destination. Then, His considerate protective nature issues urgent warnings to ensure this sacred union is protected from the destruction of premature invasion. His warning continues (*Song* 2:8-16) with expanded instruction on how to avoid the danger of slipping into the progression before that special day.

CHAPTER SEVEN

Neighborhood Watch

A few years ago, we invited everyone in our subdivision to a casual meeting to discuss some suspicious activity that had been occurring. It was evident, by the high attendance, that the concern was unanimous and that we had the beginnings of a great solution. We all had the same goals: to protect our property and to ensure the future enjoyment of our investment.

There was a certain beauty of a small community coming together with a sincere willingness to watch out for each other. A verbal agreement was made among the residents to establish a Neighborhood Watch. Together, we communicated both incidents that had occurred as well as our plans to prevent additional prohibited activities. Immediately, we put up signs similar to this: "This Community Protected by Neighborhood Watch."

The principle of community surveillance is also extremely beneficial for accountability purposes. I recognized this early on with my children. We are born into sin and if left to ourselves, sin will eventually entice us all. Our hearts are so desperately wicked that they simply can't be trusted (*Jeremiah* 17:9). Until the Holy Spirit takes up residence in the hearts of our children, there is an extra level of spiritual involvement necessary. I struggled finding the perfect balance. I still do.

For us, this meant finding people who were spiritually like-minded, whom we trusted, to lovingly mentor our daughter. We saw very early on that the curse of rebellion, and the temptation to find her own way, would be a real challenge for her. We wanted to provide her with additional resources for the same truth we were speaking to her. God has immensely blessed her with a handful of faithful women to walk alongside her on her journey to biblical womanhood.

These women are devoted to not only empowering our daughter to boldly walk with Christ, but also to purposefully prevent the devastation of sin in her life. We have not reached the point of courtship yet. But I am encouraged by the hope that we have created a strong defense to help protect her purity. Above all, we will all continue to direct her to the One, who is completely trustworthy, to safeguard her very soul.

In our neighborhood meeting, not only did we commit to watch out for each other, but the first order of business was to install a streetlight. We had all recognized that most of the suspicious activity was occurring in the darkest corner of the neighborhood, where the perpetrators assumed they were hidden. We had a strong inclination that illuminating the area of concern would deter them. Light also deters sin in our family life. I realized that even if my children did not yet possess the Holy Spirit, I did. I asked God to give me wisdom, and many times He led me to uncover certain circumstances that had the potential to be dangerous to my kids. As I prayed that their sin would not be hidden and brought to the light, I had to be prepared to respond in grace where the Lord answered.

Sin loves the dark and hates the light (*John* 3:20). This knowledge is powerful. We can find protection in the light. When our deeds are known in the light, it becomes easier to think clearly and make better choices. The darkness can give a delusion of privacy and a false sense of freedom (*Ephesians* 5:8-14). We must ensure our children have a keen awareness to their natural depravity and surround them with a community willing to shine the light of Christ to provide protection.

Protection Proposal

Our neighbors unanimously agreed to an informal proposal to aid in the protection of our community. Contacts were made, information was shared, and a beautiful alliance was formed.

It is vital that as a couple enters a relationship prior to marriage, they have a personal awareness of both their individual strengths and weaknesses, as well as opportunities and threats that may present themselves in their relationship. We can be assured that a relationship that seeks to glorify God will face spiritual warfare; and often, it will manifest itself in strong sexual temptation as the couple grows in love for each other. Resisting sexual advances can be awkwardly difficult, but preplanned responses to sensitively head them off provides another layer of protection.

We can find ourselves making large financial investments to protect our home, our health, and things we value. We can spend countless hours making certain we have fences built, security systems in place, and developing plans to efficiently pass along assets we have worked hard to accumulate. God help us to intentionally focus our efforts to establish great protections for our children and the plans that He has for them.

In our last chapter, Shulamite just spoke of the wonder of the sexual progression, then concluded with a compelling warning against stirring up sexual passion before marriage (2:1-7). This warning is so urgent that the song transitions back to a scene during courtship in which the bride-to-be had to personally apply this warning. She was prepared to act responsibly because as part of her family's watch, they had spoken truth to enlighten her to possible danger and had lovingly established boundaries for her protection.

As we investigate the way she personally embraced the teaching and safeguards that had been instituted by her family, think of springtime and a teenage boy in love. Shulamite observes her fiancé singing or calling out as he approaches his sweetheart's house.

Song of Solomon 2:8-9:
The voice of my beloved! Behold, he comes, leaping over the mountains, bounding over the hills. My beloved is like a gazelle or a young stag. Behold, there he stands behind our wall, gazing through the windows, looking through the lattice.

Using the imagery of the graceful deer-like creatures known for their sexual playfulness, she expresses admiration for his athleticism. No doubt she is privately enjoying the sexual attraction she feels for him. She thinks his behavior is adorable and is flattered by his excitement for her. They are in love and they are not hiding it.

As I consider the next verses, I think of the movie *Bambi*, after the fresh spring rain and all the flowers are popping up, and the baby animals are beginning to notice each other and fall in love. Thumper is twitter-pated, and he is flapping his foot and hearts are floating all around him and his bunny love.

Song of Solomon 2:10-13
My beloved speaks and says to me: "Arise, my love, my beautiful one, and come away, for behold, the winter is past; the rain is over and gone. The flowers appear on the earth, the time of singing has come, and the voice of the turtledove is heard in our land. The fig tree ripens its figs, and the vines are in blossom; they give forth fragrance. Arise, my love, my beautiful one, and come away.

Solomon is proclaiming, "This is the season of love. Come out and let me romance you." He definitely wants his betrothed to cross the wall that is separating them, come out, and spend time with him.

Notice the word "love" in verses 10 and 13. The Hebrew word *dod* means lover (my darling) and has a strong sexual connotation. He declares winter is over and spring has arrived. The figs are ripening on the tree, the turtle doves are making their nests, so it must be the time for us to make our nest or to make love. You can feel it in the air.

He could be saying, "I want you so badly I can't wait another day. Let's get married now." He continues to back up his case.

Song of Solomon 2:14
O my dove, in the clefts of the rock, in the crannies of the cliff, let me see your face, let me hear your voice, for your voice is sweet, and your face is lovely.

Turtle doves are considered to be lovebirds. Solomon implies she is the lovebird he should be mating with, but she is way up high hiding in the clefts of the rock. She is somewhere behind that wall in the secret places of the stairs, and he cannot even see her. So, he pleads with her, "I want to hear your voice and see your form or your figure." The language indicates he is expressing sexual desire.

He is pretty convincing, isn't he? It is not, "Come on, we'll hang out." He is enticing her, promising their time together will be romantic.

An engaged couple should long to be able to express their sexual passion. They should intensely desire to be with one another. This is normal. If an engaged couple is not experiencing sexual desire, something is not lining up and the issue should be addressed.

There is—and should be—physical attraction, but courtship is a season where a couple intentionally observes the character of a person enough to nail down that marriage with this person is an acceptable option. It is the time to discover a partner's dreams and their struggles, to enjoy being with them, to engage in deep conversations, and really get to know each other.

Too often unmarried couples allow sexual desire to distract them from the essentialness of really getting to know each other, but Shulamite uses a metaphor to wisely express her concern.

Song of Solomon 2:15
Take us the foxes, the little foxes, that spoil the vines: for our vines have tender grapes.

Foxes come into a vineyard, dig holes, and loosen the dirt around the vine. This hinders the health and growth of the vine. So, the families of the vine keeper diligently watch for these little creatures and even sleep outside to protect their vineyards from the pesky foxes.

Remember in Chapter One, the bride referred to her body and complexion as a vineyard. She is admitting the desire for her fiancé is strong; but, at the same time, she is warning him to be cautious and protect her virginity in the same way a vine-keeper protects the delicate young grapes from these little foxes that destroy the tender vines. This girl was sensitive to express a longing for her man but, at the same time, bold to remind him they could not go there. They could not go there yet; but as her husband-to-be, he should be eager and willing to protect her virginity. This is a valid test for the relationship. If a guy is not willing to respect her desire for purity and shoulder that responsibility, the couple should back off in the relationship. This vividly backs up the warning from verse 7. *Do not stir up or awaken love until it pleases* or until you are married.

The urge for sexual activity between an engaged couple is extremely strong and even more difficult to resist; but for the sake of lasting and fulfilling marital sex, God pleads with singles to resist the temptation to stir up the passion before the wedding night. In this scene, God stresses the need to be aware the temptation will come and to be prepared to resist. It is common that the female will need to issue the warning lovingly but firmly. What a great passage for a mom to use to encourage her daughter ahead of time to be prepared to resist! Your daughter needs to realize the only way she can resist is to have a supreme respect for God. Philip Ryken says, "Practicing celibacy is not simply refraining from sex; it is an active and positive way of offering ourselves to God." [59]

Some girls may fear that resisting will cause the fiancé or boyfriend to be frustrated or to even reject the relationship. Leslie Vernick warns, "Fear can paralyze us or propel us into foolish action. We need to guard our heart against the fear perpetrated by an overactive imagination that tends to always picture the worst-case scenario. God instructs us to deal with our fears by trusting him."[60] In this narrative, Solomon responded as a God-honoring believer by agreeing with her warning and showing respect that she would stand

---

[59] Ryken, *Love of Loves in the Song of Songs*, 76.
[60] Leslie Vernick, *How to Act Right When Your Spouse Acts Wrong*, (New York, New York: Waterbrook, 2001), 79.

strong on her convictions. How a couple navigates this sexual urgency is a major test of whether a couple will dedicate their marriage journey to the glory of the Lord.

The grammar in verse nine is also interesting because the bride-to-be says "take us" or catch us the little foxes. The request is plural.[61] Hey, people, help us catch the little foxes. We need your help. It is as though she is asking that her family and the community join them in the effort to protect their purity.

Ian Duguid points out that the bride-to-be says Solomon is standing behind "our wall." The wall belongs to her family. It is a wall of protection. Her purity is not just her individual decision or plan but a family plan (*Song* 8:8-10).[62]

Parents and family should be involved. They know the couple better than anyone else and they care about their future. The sex drive is strong and young couples need loving help.

This brings up the question: how do young couples protect their blossoming love until marriage? How can families and friends help? We often hear that couples need to construct proper boundaries that include a lot of rules. Ian Duguid warns: "Expect yourselves to be very weak, and so don't put yourselves in situations in which the temptation will be overwhelming."[63]

Wise boundaries include both avoiding sexual touch and committing to never be alone in a secluded place. For children still living in the home, parents can and should oversee the budding relationship. Parents can explain to the young man how they expect their daughter to be treated. They can require that doors in the home remain open. Parents can request that the man explain where the couple is going, what they will be doing, who will be with them and when they will return. I know families that send another brother or sister along when a couple has plans that do not involve a group setting. The temptation to succumb to uncontrolled passion seems to diminish when someone else is present. Planning family activities that include the prospective spouse allows parents to observe character

---

[61] Ryken, *Love of Loves in the Song of Songs*, 70.
[62] Duguid, *Song of Songs*, 44.
[63] Duguid, *Song of Songs*, 49.

traits and involve the prospect in conversations about family values. The most important dialogue will be those that confirm and encourage the man's faith and walk with Christ. When a young man sees the value of the girl he is pursuing, he will respect parents who want to ensure her emotional and physical well-being.

The problem with the boundary approach alone is our humanness (depravity) tends to look for loopholes or label our situations as "exceptions." Because lust is a desire that is out of control, it can overpower rules. We have to train our hearts by reinforcing the reasons for the rule.

This is the approach taken here in the *Song*. The reason the *Song* teaches to wait sexually is so that a couple can present their vineyard in full bloom of marriage to enjoy each other without regret or remorse. Remaining sexually pure is trusting that God's plan is best.

God issues the warning because He loves and wants to protect from future pain and bless with His absolute best. He can be trusted.

Just like the vine keeper protects against foxes and then waits for the vineyard to produce luscious grapes that can be enjoyed, lovers must watch over their vineyards and wait until they are in full bloom of marriage before making love. Couples who regularly remind themselves of the reason they are waiting to have sexual intimacy will have an easier time respecting the boundaries they have established.

Some couples hesitate to bring up potential areas of conflict, but I love what Shulamite confidently declares after they address their little foxes:

Song of Solomon 2:16
My beloved is mine, and I am his: he grazes among the lilies.

The Shulamite declares their relationship is solid. They belong to each other. They are a unit. The difficult conversation actually strengthened the relationship.

The concluding imagery is powerful. She still admires him as a graceful, athletic stud who is lingering to feed among the lilies. This is the same imagery she uses in Chapter Five to compare his lips to a bed of lilies. So, the language could possibly indicate that he is kissing her lips goodbye or at least desiring to. He respects her convictions.

She is affirming that she also deeply desires him, but it is not time yet to consummate the relationship. So, she bids her beloved farewell with this same thrilled admiration she had when he arrived:

Song of Solomon 2:17
Until the day breathes and the shadows flee, turn, my beloved, be like a gazelle or a young stag on cleft mountains.

Despite her longing for him, the time for love has not arrived. So, she reluctantly, but firmly says until another day when morning comes, and the shadows disappear, he will have to "turn" or leave. As Iain Duguid states, "Her 'no' is a 'not quite yet, my love', rather than a 'never.'"[64]

This is such a sweet and gentle way to show she desires her man and wants to please him. At the same time, God's way is more urgently important and worth waiting for.

There is a truth here that is even sweeter. Christians have a greater and more perfect lover who desires us so passionately that He literally came to this earth and shed His blood that we might become His bride. We are watching and waiting for our Groom to return and escort us to the marriage supper of the Lamb. In the meantime, He is calling us to tend our vineyards in holiness and sanctification. He even sent His Spirit to help us.

If you cannot declare of the Heavenly Bridegroom, "My beloved is mine and I am His," then don't let your sin, your fear or your brokenness keep you from arising and answering His call to come. Don't let your attempts to be good enough keep you away. No one will ever be good enough. We enter a relationship with Him based solely on

---

[64] Duguid, *Song of Songs*, 45.

what He has done for us. Salvation is by grace and grace alone and His grace calls out to you, *"Arise, my darling, my beautiful one, and come away."* [65]

---

[65] The thoughts expressed here of responding to the call to arise and come away as a response to Christ are credited to Ian Duguid in *Song of Songs*, 52.

CHAPTER EIGHT

Repurpose Regret

"Some Christian mothers admit they delay sex education at home because of the shame they feel from their own past."[66] I would venture to guess this is accurate for most of us. Can you see how the enemy is working behind the scenes? I see him silently pulling each generation into the darkness. When we have determined to "find out for ourselves," we follow the enemy and walk right in. He essentially closes the door behind us and attempts to keep us locked up with guilt and shame. Every time we get up the courage to crack the door open to take in some light, he reminds us of our sin and we become too ashamed to escape.

There is a way out. A way back into the light.

Repentance leads to truth and truth leads to freedom. God stands ready to grant complete and perfect forgiveness. However, His plan includes not only repentance but glorifying Him as the Redeemer so that others will also be drawn to the gift of redemption. We glorify Him by vulnerably confessing the truth of our brokenness and gratefully declaring how His grace has specifically changed our lives and freed us from the bondage of sin.

---

[66]Nancy DeMoss Wolgemuth, *Lies Women Believe*, (Chicago, IL: Moody Publishing, 2018), 132.

Many times God instructed His children to remember what He had done for them and how He had brought them out of bondage (*Deuteronomy* 6:12 and *Ephesians* 2:12-13). If it was important for His children then, it also applies to believers now. We have been given many examples of how God has taken broken, sinful humans and redeemed them for His glorious purposes (*Galations* 1 and *Luke* 19). He can do the same with us! I truly believe, just as we learn from biblical accounts, our children can also learn from our mistakes. We encourage you to fight the enemy by allowing God to use your past sins to protect the next generation.

My husband and I have determined to be transparent with our children. We are grateful that we recognized early on that the pressure of perfection is not helpful. Yes, God does demand holiness. But, we are only capable of holy living through the power of Christ; it is not possible in our own strength. We are finding that God opens many doors for us to share the gospel when we choose to be honest about our brokenness. This transparency is not only essential with our own children, but also with others who cross our paths.

Just as we may find it is time to clean out our closets as the seasons change, we can be mindful when seasons of repentance are necessary. My husband and I did not drop all of our sinful pasts onto our kids at one time. That would not have been fruitful or kind. However, in obedience, we prayerfully asked God to reveal to us the right time. He has been faithful not only to direct our discussions, but also to supply sufficient grace for each occasion. Confessing sin is never easy. It is especially difficult to share with someone who looks up to you. Of course, we want our kids to only think the best of us. What if the "best of us" is our story of redemption?

God's plan is perfect; we are not. He knew that we would never be able to live a life of complete holiness, so He provided holiness for us. In whatever way it may be that you find you have fallen short, let us remind you that it is never too late for God to redeem. It is what He does. Through Christ, He redeems and restores. If He can redeem my story, I am confident He can do the same for yours.

One of the ways I have personally experienced redemption is through allowing Him to use my failures. Ultimately, my daughter's (children's) choices will be her (their) own. But, our words of warning and instruction become more powerful when they are shared in humility alongside real-life consequences that can be seen: "No matter what kind of sexual sin you may have struggled with, the cross is where we may each find mercy, cleansing, and redemption."[67]

The enemy will become powerless over our sexuality when we truly grasp how it directly relates to our spirituality. "From the very beginning, God intended human sexuality and marriage to be a picture of the gospel."[68] His redemptive plan can be traced all throughout scripture.

Redeemed, Restored, and Refreshed

Some moms may be reading this with heavy hearts because they or their daughters have already crossed the line. Navigating the exploded mine field with her will require supernatural tenderness and directional hope. That is why Jesus died. He took our shame, our guilt, and our regrets into His soul and exchanged them for His righteousness and purity. He bore the punishment for every act of lust and rebellion exuding out of a believer's heart. He suffered so that a female who despised the gift of virginity could start over and become a refreshed and reoriented Christian who is washed clean. The scars remain in the heart to remind us of His priceless scars, but our lives can be resurrected to the liberty of forgiveness and a fresh start.

1 John 1:9
If we confess our sins, he is faithful and just to forgive us our sins and to cleanse us from all unrighteousness.

---

[67] Wolgemuth, *Lies Women Believe*, 141.
[68] Wolgemuth, *Lies Women Believe*, 140-142.

On Mother's Day, our pastor challenged moms to be vulnerable and honest about who we really are before our children. I cannot give them my heart if I am protecting an image, if I am concerned about what others think. My failure in front of them is part of the plan because it is not about being a great mom but a gospel mom. A gospel mom admits mistakes and takes them to the cross where she receives forgiveness and grace to turn her life back to the direction of Christ. When a child can hear that her mom understands the error of her past and has been empowered to move forward in grace, hope, and confidence in God, she will desire and trust a Redeemer like that. I am not saying we need to divulge details of our past. The amount of detail depends on the prompting of the Spirit. Our daughters need to know part of the reason we can speak with such confidence is that God in His grace used our failures to point us to a better way, the right way, His way.

So, if you feel your past disqualifies you from training your daughter in righteous sex, realize that grace requalifies you. The truth, when combined with gospel, never loses its power.

Your daughter may be the one struggling with the guilt of promiscuity. The same grace is available to her. She also has the opportunity to proceed with a redeemed life and be washed white as snow (See Appendix B). Is release to a fresh new life even a biblical concept for someone so broken? How did Jesus respond to women who had committed sexual sin?[69]

Ian Duguid explains:

> He never shamed these people or condemned them for their sin; indeed, He was willing to have His own reputation reviled in order to provide them with

---

[69] Jesus invited the adulterous woman at the well to abandon her lifestyle of promiscuity and to replace it with worship. (John 4:23b-24)
Jesus assured the repentant woman caught in the act of adultery that He did not condemn her but instead directed her to a fresh start (John 8:11b-12).
When the promiscuous woman washed the feet of Jesus with her tears, He graciously accepted her act of repentance, defended her actions, and blessed her (Luke 7:48b, 50b)

cleansing, acceptance, a new life and a new hope...Bring your broken sexual history to Jesus, whatever its exact nature—lust, pornography, the pursuit of same-sex desires, premarital sex, adultery, or some other sin. Bring it to the foot of the cross and lay it down there. Let God nail it to the cross with Jesus Christ, as part of the record of sins that He died for, and that He paid for in full. Then hear the glorious words that Jesus says about your sin: "It is finished." It is paid for. It is done away with. You are set free to learn to truly love your brothers and your sisters. You are released to live life, to continue to wrestle against temptation, sometimes winning perhaps often losing, but always looking to the cross as your only hope in life and death.[70]

Lorraine Pintus explains that cleansing ourselves from past sexual sin is much like taking a shower:

First, we get rid of the old, like we remove dirty clothes before showering. Next, we step under the water and allow God's forgiveness to pour over us and wash our past down the drain. Finally, we put on new, clean garments which the Bible calls clothing ourselves in the righteousness of Christ (2 Corinthians 5:21; Galatians 3:27)...Just be honest with God. Admit to Him everything you've done—He already knows it anyway. Tell Him you were wrong and grieved over your sin.[71]

I relate to Lorraine's illustration. I particularly remember a time when the Holy Spirit convicted me of a sin—I don't even remember the exact sin; but I do remember being in the shower, crying and confessing my self-seeking behavior. I was totally open with the Lord. I

---

[70] Duguid, *Song of Songs*, 141.
[71] Dillow and Pintus, *Intimate issues*, 82-83.

remember the sincere longing to experience His love and acceptance. He was so faithful. That was the most refreshing shower I ever stood under.

Acts 3:19-20
Repent therefore, and turn back, that your sins may be blotted out, that times of refreshing may come from the presence of the Lord, and that he may send the Christ appointed for you, Jesus.

Later in personal study, I landed on *Acts* 3:19-20. Because of my recent experience, I could embrace the genuine effects of this directive and its promise. Times of refreshing are the most vividly accurate way of describing the results of God's forgiveness. I knew I was in the presence of the Lord that day. I realize this verse is a plea to turn from sin for salvation; but as a Christian, who had once again miserably failed, the joy of my salvation was restored to me when I intentionally and with all my being turned from the sin I confessed. When I was confessing my sin in the shower that day, what I wanted was God—His presence. I was not concerned about what anyone else thought. I wanted Him. I return to this blessed truth whenever I find myself straying. I believe part of the refreshing is that fresh start. We may carry scars from the past sin, but they serve as reminders of the scars on His hands and how much He loves us.

For mothers or daughters who have sexual sin in their past or maybe in their present, there is promise of a fresh start. Anyone can be released from the bondage of sexual guilt and shame to a new different lifestyle (See Appendix B). After sincere repentance, after turning away from the wrong behavior and embracing God, she can claim that day as a marker, the date she determined to pursue God above lust. She has freedom to admit her disobedient past, while rejoicing that it is nailed to the cross of Christ. Her life from that point forward becomes a joyful pursuit of holiness.

I do not want to paint a picture that arriving at this point or moving on from this point is easy. Although a fresh start is simple, it can still be extremely painful. Sexual sin is different from other sins because it involves our bodies. The complication of the problem is that sexual sin makes you one with another person physically, emotionally, and spiritually.[72] The ties that still exist must be broken. The ties could be a current relationship that must reach an immediate understanding that sexual desire can no longer be stirred up with conversation, touch, or behavior.

The Shulamite had a family wall of protection to shield her from the temptation to stir passion before the wedding night. A similar commitment to avoid secluded visits may be necessary to break the tie. If the current relationship involves an unbeliever or same-sex attraction, the gospel change in behavior must be declared; and the sexual ties must be completely severed. This may seem scary difficult; but when we determine to openly speak truth in love, the Lord anoints the explanation.

Sometimes the emotional ties are as strong as chains. They can haunt the one who has confessed the sin. These ties are broken through the expulsive power of a greater affection.[73] Strive to replace the memories with fascinating truths of Christ's overcoming love. Worship your way into His presence.

The new journey can feel like a crawl. Strong chains may require the consistent intervention of a faithful friend or counselor. Their encouragement and direction should be centered on the life-giving power of the gospel. We highly recommend pouring yourself into Bible Study (See Resources: *Release from Sexual Bondage* in Appendix B).

Be encouraged. The new journey is a fresh start with a new beauty. The gifts of confession and forgiveness usher in the hope of a brighter future. On her wedding day, Shulamite was able to admit her culturally unacceptable flaws (skin darkened by the sun) and direct attention to loveliness.

Song of Solomon 1:5-6
I am very dark, but lovely, O daughters of Jerusalem, like the tents of Kedar, like the curtains of Solomon. Do not gaze at me because I am

---

[72] 1 *Corinthians* 6:15-18.
[73] https://www.kevinhalloran.net/the-expulsive-power-of-a-new-affection-by-thomas-chalmers-an-11-quote-summary/

dark, because the sun has looked upon me. My mother's sons were angry with me; they made me keeper of the vineyards, but my own vineyard I have not kept!

In the same way, those who are forgiven receive new beauty from Christ. *Isaiah 61:3* proclaims Jesus comes:

> *...to grant to those who mourn in Zion—to give them a beautiful headdress instead of ashes, the oil of gladness instead of mourning, the garment of praise instead of a faint spirit; that they may be called oaks of righteousness, the planting of the LORD, that he may be glorified.*

He transforms regret and sin scars of those who were previously captive to sin and shame into beauty and gladness that glorify Him.

CONCLUSION

God's Endorsement

We can find rest in God's truth. Confidence is a gift He offers us when we choose to walk in obedience and trust in His sovereignty. We do not have to question His approval if we have received His Righteousness. I cannot walk this out for my daughter, and I cannot be the Holy Spirit for her. I do not have to. What a relief!

We can trust God with our children. He allows us to be involved in their lives, but it is His desire for them to have a personal relationship with the One that brought them into existence. The very act of love that gave them life is often the subject we neglect to trust Him with.

God has not promised that our daughters will not make mistakes. I have found that I tend to be superstitious. There were times when I thought if I did all the "right" things (i.e. go to church, read my Bible, etc.), God would protect my children. I was brought to my knees many times before I recognized this did not line up with His character. Although He has not promised us a pain-free life, He has promised only good for those who love Him and are called according to His purposes (*Romans* 8:28). This is the motivation we need to ensure our children are taught the gospel. Our desire should be that they may "believe in the name of the Son of God that you (they) may know that you (they) have eternal life" (*1 John* 5:13).

Solomon and the Shulamite's story did not end with the conclusion of Chapter 8. Although we can be assured the plan for romance and marriage given in the *Song of Solomon* is given to us from God Himself, Solomon endured pain and suffering later in life as he veered off the path God had laid for him. At the end of his life, he realized, "But all this I laid to heart, examining it all, how the righteous and the wise and their deeds are in the hand of God" (*Ecclesiastes* 9:1). We should not get discouraged when we find that the "formula" we were following does not produce the results we had envisioned. Like Solomon, we can learn many things good for ourselves and useful to others.[74]

God's plan and instructions for sexual intimacy profoundly display the many facets of His character. This allows communication with your daughter to be driven by worship. The way He designed humans, emotionally and physically, to experience delight and bonding through physical intimacy highlights His brilliance as creator. The power of relationship between husband and wife magnifies His concept of love. The picture of Christ as our Bridegroom proves His sensitivity and caring nature. It reminds us how deeply He desires communion with us. To top all that off, God's realization that we will sometimes fail to follow His design demonstrates the heart of a perfect Father. He understands our weaknesses and provides forgiveness to relieve our guilt and shame. He graciously illuminates a path for future blessings. His Word is dependable. Worshipping through the truths with your daughter will provide the confidence you need for this delicate subject. Worshipping with you will provide the incentive your daughter needs to move in the right direction without fear. She can trust God with this aspect of her life.

---

[74] *Ecclesiastes 9:1. Mathew Henry Commentary.*
https://biblehub.com/commentaries/ecclesiastes/9-1.htm

God's Blessing

The sweetness of God's character is also displayed in His approval of the physical act of marital love. Once Solomon enters the paradise of his bride's garden and declares the exhilaration of their wedding night experience (*Song of Solomon* 4—See Epilogue), a third party (presumably God Himself) encourages the couple to enjoy His gift of sex to the max.

Song of Solomon 5:1c
Eat, friends, drink, and be drunk with love!

God records that Solomon prepares his son for marriage by emphasizing the supreme pleasure God intends in *Proverbs* 5:18-19:

> *Let your fountain be blessed, and rejoice in the wife of your youth, lovely deer, a graceful doe. Let her breasts fill you at all times with delight; be intoxicated always in her love.*

Also notable in Solomon's final words of exhortation to God's people, when he contemplates both his successes and failures, he urges them:

> *Enjoy life with the wife whom you love, all the days of your vain life (Ecclesiastes 9:9).*

Solomon is saying, "Cling to that special mate God gives you for your entire life. Don't be distracted by other partners. Find supreme pleasure in your spouse."

God blessed us with the gift of sex. He endorses the pleasure of it inside the marriage relationship. We are praying for you as you point your daughters to embrace the sacred gift of sex as He intended, to reserve it for their future husband, then enjoy it all their married life.

EPILOGUE

Awaken, My Love!

Preparing your daughter for marriage is so much more than verbalizing incentives and warnings to remain pure. It is a lifetime of conversations that also include the glories of God's plan for sex. Each conversation increases in information and confirmation. Then, it seems all of a sudden, your daughter is ready to be married and needs more intensive instruction. God's word provides that for you.

The wedding night is monumental. Moments of great significance can often cause great apprehension, especially for virgins. A mother who is willing to be vulnerable and transparent with details can greatly relieve her daughter's anxiety.

I had the privilege of interviewing a young bride about her precious memories from the special night her mother took her to a hotel room to pray and offer sexual advice for the soon approaching honeymoon:

> *Debbie:* "What did you find helpful when your Mom took you on the overnight mother-daughter dinner and hotel night the week before you got married?"
> *Sara*: "First of all, my mom, my sister and I are best friends. We already talked about everything. She always answered our questions. She had our first real

mother-daughter talk when our breasts started to develop, and she bought us our first bra. She explained how our bodies would be changing and how hormones might affect the way we felt, what to expect when our menstrual cycle started.

Our parents trained us for purity. My dad gave us purity rings when we turned twelve. They protected us by insisting we always have a chaperone. They explained the beauty of married union and how sacred it was, urged us to remain pure; but at the same time, they assured us that no matter what, even if we lost our purity, they would love us and care for us. They made me want to be pure—not just for me and my future husband, but also for them. I was very confident that my parents loved each other, so that helped a lot too.

The premarital training lessons helped too because you were open; and it provided my then fiancé, soon to be husband and me a specific opportunity to talk without dwelling on the intimate thoughts all the time.[75] It proved to be perfect timing to talk without dwelling on it.

Mom talked with my sister and me all the time and was willing to answer any question; but that night before I got married, she got much more detailed. Of course, it helped because we grew up around animals. She described ways I could make my husband happy, even during the times, for health reasons, I might not be able to fully participate[76]. She explained I might feel a little pain the first few times, but not to get discouraged. She gave me a large makeup bag with lubricant, hand towels, and mints.

---

[75] PreparingforPartnership.org
[76] Non-contagious health reasons that might prevent a wife from fully participating in sex include the menstrual cycle or injury to a part of the body that would limit activity or positioning.

> Because of some health problems from my past, my body had a hard time opening up and adjusting to intimacy the first month. This upset me. I felt very comfortable talking with my mom. She arranged an appointment with a gynecologist to confirm I was ok. I was encouraged and after that, my body adjusted. I am so grateful my mom was so easy to talk to, and I knew she cared."

What a gift to this young bride! Her mother saw the preciousness of the physical union that was approaching for her daughter and her soon to be husband. She gently and lovingly prepared her for that special honeymoon night. Our prayer is that the thoughts in this Appendix will offer you some thoughts you can gift to your daughter before she gives herself fully to the man with whom she has chosen to spend the rest of her life.

According to Linda Dillow, the most important sexual organ is your mind. She quotes Dr. Douglas Rosenau, theologian, and Christian sex therapist, "Sex is 80 percent imagination and mind and 20 percent friction."[77] It is not just your thoughts in the bedroom, but also your thoughts throughout your day that determine how you will respond to your husband's sexual advances. In Chapters Five and Six of this book, we unpacked the verses in *Song of Solomon* 1 where the couple lovingly and positively conversed throughout the wedding day and at the wedding feast. Their minds were occupied (consumed) with praise-filled thoughts for their spouse. These thoughts compelled them to vocalize and act later that evening. The bride voiced her approval of Solomon's character, physique, and sexual skill. This prepared her mind so that later Solomon could gently prepare her body. *Song of Solomon* 2:1-6 hints at the beauty of that first honeymoon night, but Chapter Four illuminates the wonder of it.

As we dive into Chapter Four of *The Song* and work our way through the dialogue, notice the communication. The wife is not consumed with self and how she looks or performs. She concentrates

---

[77] Dillow and Pintus, *Intimate Issues,* 23.

on the delight she finds in her husband. Solomon opens the chapter by declaring the beauty of his bride. She receives his compliments. She does not feign modesty by correcting his statement. She is his standard of beauty, and there is no need for her to compare herself with other women. She allows him, without interruption, to describe her features that he finds attractive. This passage unveils the details of the progression that were briefly outlined in Chapter Two of the *Song*. Remember the progression is God's intended way to prepare the wife's body, and it begins with sincere praise.

Song of Solomon 4:1-2
Behold, you are beautiful, my love, behold, you are beautiful! Your eyes are doves behind your veil. Your hair is like a flock of goats leaping down the slopes of Gilead. Your teeth are like a flock of shorn ewes that have come up from the washing, all of which bear twins and not one among them has lost its young.

The groom is gazing into his bride's eyes. They reflect the gentleness and purity of a dove. She must be entranced by his eyes also. Because she has fixed her mind on the traits she admires about her groom, her eyes shine with the wonder that he is her gift from God. The wonder infers an innocence. This could also be a reference to her virginity. He is sincere in comparing her eyes to a dove.

In a sensitive effort to make her feel more comfortable in the overwhelming grandeur of the palace, he describes her hair and teeth by using metaphors this country girl is familiar with. Her long soft flowing hair reminds him of the long-haired goats gracefully descending the rugged mountain. The wool from their hair was exquisite and expensive. He contrasts the dark hair of the goats with the whiteness of freshly washed sheep. Not only are her teeth sparkling white, but they are perfectly balanced in pairs around her mouth.

Song of Solomon 4:3
Your lips are like a scarlet thread, and your mouth is lovely. Your cheeks are like halves of a pomegranate behind your veil.

The bride must have applied lip color because her groom is voicing his approval. He looks past the shimmer of her wedding veil to comment that her cheeks have a rosy appearance like the inside color of a pomegranate that has been split in half. He is putting her at ease and granting her security as he expresses personal delight in the features of her face. The bride gracefully receives these comments. Instead of denying her beauty, she concentrates on how blessed she is to have a man that expresses approval.

Song of Solomon 4:4
Your neck is like the tower of David, built in rows of stone; on it hang a thousand shields, all of them shields of warriors.

He continues to slowly lower his gaze, appreciating every feature, proving to his bride that he loves every inch of who she is. Comparing her neck to the tower of David seems to be a reference to her dignified posture. Dillow and Pintus break down the analogy: "Her neck spoke of her erect and queenly carriage and symbolized what she was to her husband: a source of strength and encouragement."[78]

Solomon acknowledges this aspect of her character that shows up in her posture. He is entering the sexual progression with sincere appreciation and gratitude, backing up his approval of her physical features with references to her outstanding character. He skillfully avoids the common pitfall where a woman feels like all her husband cares about is sex. He obviously cares about her as a person.

Solomon advances the progression as he once again lowers his gaze.

Song of Solomon 4:5
Your two breasts are like two fawns, twins of a gazelle, that graze among the lilies.

The fawns of a gazelle are young, graceful, deer-like creatures known for their sexual playfulness. I think of gazing across a meadow

---
[78] Dillow and Pintus, *Intimacy Ignited*, 135.

and experiencing a sense of enchantment as I note the wonder of two frolicking, perfectly matched fawns. Dillow and Pintus connect the lilies mentioned here with 5:13 where the bride describes Solomon's lips as lilies. He could be so swept up in the wonder of his gaze that he finds himself touching his lips to her breasts with kisses. The description conveys appreciation for a beauty that is natural. No matter what the exact imagery is suggesting, God is granting holy liberty to find pleasure in your spouse's body. This charming description reveals the heart of a creator who desires His creatures find allure and wonder in love. We were wonderfully designed to long for such a relationship. It is worth waiting for and preparing for.

Song of Solomon 4:6
Until the day breathes and the shadows flee, I will go away to the mountain of myrrh and the hill of frankincense.

Solomon assures his bride that he is not in a hurry. He is willing to take all night to pause along the journey to appreciate each feature of her body. He is not taking her for granted but is expressing affirmation and acceptance of her entire being. The mountain of myrrh and the hill of frankincense refer to the destination of his bodily journey.

Song of Solomon 4:7
You are altogether beautiful, my love; there is no flaw in you.

Of course, the bride has flaws and imperfections. She pointed them out and named them in Chapter One. A number of brides-to-be have expressed nervousness at the thought of disrobing on their wedding night in front of their new husband. Imperfections are embarrassing when we obsess over them. With age, the imperfections grow and increase in number. How is it possible to love someone who has unattractive features? God's intention is that both spouses be focused on the fact that He gave us a precious gift to one another. I think of the movie, "Wonder." When Julia Robert's baby was born with what most would consider a grotesque birth defect, she received him as absolutely adorable. She could declare this wholeheartedly because he belonged to her. The entire family adored him. He was a gift to them from God. That is why God explains in *1 Corinthians* 7:4 that the husband and wife have authority or ownership of the body of their spouse. We unconditionally accept and love what belongs to us. Throughout the *Song*, Solomon claims his wife as "my Love." Shulamite refers to her husband as "my Beloved." In 6:3, the bride confidently declares, *"I am my beloved's and my beloved is mine."* In 7:10, she announces, *"I am my beloved's, and his desire is for me."*

This is a way of life exemplified by Jesus who sincerely loves ugly beings like us with undying love. We are a gift to Him from the Father (*John* 17:11). The very character of Jesus is love, and we have the capacity to love with "blind" eyes through Him. His story becomes our narrative. Iain Duguid explains, "if you begin to find your security and significance in the Lord, you will start to be freed to delight in the unique ways in which the Lord has gifted your spouse and fitted her or him for you."[79]

Solomon receives his bride as a gift; therefore, he genuinely does not notice flaws. What hope and instruction for marriage! This is another endorsement of avoiding the progression until the wedding night because only after covenant vows are spoken before God does a husband and wife actually and completely belong to each other.

Solomon is not concerned about self. He positioned to fully concentrate on his bride and celebrate her uniqueness because he views her as his prized possession. He recognizes she is a precious gift to him. Likewise, when the bride concentrates on Solomon's traits and features, she loses herself in the delight of pleasing him. The best way your daughter can prepare herself to love as magnificently as this is to abandon herself to the pursuit of God now. She will find the freedom to view her future husband as a precious gift.

---

[79] Duguid, *Song of Songs,* 77.

Song of Solomon 4:8
Come with me from Lebanon, my bride; come with me from Lebanon. Depart from the peak of Amana, from the peak of Senir and Hermon, from the dens of lions, from the mountains of leopards.

Now isn't this odd? In the middle of a romantic evening that is building in passion, he presents an invitation to travel with him. Every commentary we read had a different interpretation and explanation. So, knowing the minds of females, and considering the whirlwind events of the bride's past week, we agree with Dillow and Pintus. We believe that Solomon is gently convincing his homesick bride to set aside her thoughts of home and join his thoughts of their relationship.

Why would Solomon pause in the middle of this passionate progression to speak of Lebanon and mountain peaks and lion dens? During the past few days, since arriving at the palace, Shulamite has encountered a totally different world that she must claim as her new normal. She left the familiarity of a modest country home, traveled through the wilderness by extravagant means in a pompous parade (*Song of Solomon* 3:6-11), (as the center of attention) and landed in the luxurious palace full of the inquisitive stares of a multitude of princesses. Next, was the wedding. Then, the formal banquet. Now she is in the bridal chamber with the king. She is trying to digest this while she offers intimate attention to the king. Whose thoughts would not wander? It is not uncommon, at the end of the day when a female is unwinding and finds herself on the precious path of romance, for her thoughts to veer slightly off the path of romance into random thoughts. It is part of de-stressing, of letting go of the day. The mind vacillates from thought to thought until they are dismissed. One young wife told us she could find herself in a very passionate moment and, suddenly, become distracted because she notices dust on the post of the bed. She automatically instructs herself to make a note to dust the next day. She did not intentionally direct her mind that way; her thoughts just landed on a responsibility.

Solomon, who is a picture of Jesus, understands the emotional needs of his bride. He does not get frustrated, but instead, gently and poetically shifts her attention away from her thoughts of the attractions of her home country she left behind and invites her to steer her thoughts to the beauty of their moment. No wonder she has been impressed with his sensitivity. Not only did Solomon understand the importance of sensitivity, but God, the inspiration of the *Song*, wants husbands to be reminded that love is patient and sensitive. Your daughter can trust a God with such compassionate understanding. He speaks truths to couples in order to enhance their sexual lives and in doing so He brilliantly displays the depth of care He has for believers.

As Solomon invites his new wife to release her thoughts and to concentrate on their journey of love, the couple is on the edge of explicit sexual activity. This is the first time in the *Song* that Solomon refers to his love as "my bride." This term emphasizes the covenantal marriage relationship that is now official. He is gently reminding her that she has a new home with him now. The text supports the scriptural principle that sexual intercourse is reserved for marriage.

Notice how Solomon lures the attention of his bride back to the intensity of their lovemaking.

Song of Solomon 4:9-10
You have captivated my heart, my sister, my bride; you have captivated my heart with one glance of your eyes, with one jewel of your necklace. How beautiful is your love, my sister, my bride! How much better is your love than wine, and the fragrance of your oils than any spice!

He declares he is enslaved by her beauty. She has captured his entire being. He proclaims the wonder of her love. The word for love is the same word she used in Chapter One, verse two. It refers to her skill as a lover, and that it is her touches and caresses that stimulate him. He even repeats her original phrase that love is better than wine. He is intoxicated by her sensuous strokes. Point out to your daughter how pleasing the soft caresses are. Not only is her love better than wine, but the fragrance of the natural moisture produced by her sexual glands is more pleasing to him than any spice.

Solomon has squelched any insecurity or distraction by praising her sexual skill and by affirming his delight in her participation. The bride is now completely engaged. She is concentrating on pleasing her man as she responds to his attention.

Note: The bride is not Solomon's actual sister. This is a term of endearment that expresses fondness and close relationship.

Song of Solomon 4:11
Your lips drip nectar, my bride; honey and milk are under your tongue; the fragrance of your garments is like the fragrance of Lebanon.

The passion continues to build. Solomon finds such supreme pleasure in the taste of her kisses that he draws from the language God uses to describe the Promised Land.[80] He feels absolutely blessed to enter marriage with his new wife and sees her as a gift he possesses for his very own. Philip Ryken uses a quote from Doug O' Donnell to highlight the beauty of this perspective. He defines sexual intercourse:

> "...an inexplicable act of mutual possession, passion and submission: I give my total self to you, and you give your total self to me." Marriage is the only place where a man and a woman belong to one another sexually, which is not a license for abuse but an invitation to paradise.[81]

Solomon's wording proves the bride is not passive but is actively participating. She is passionately kissing and stroking him. Your daughter needs to know she should not just lie still and wait for something to happen. Her participation enhances the journey.

Solomon makes sure his bride realizes that he is appreciating every detail of their experience. He even compliments her negligee. Dillow and Pintus explain:

> The way the garment displayed Tirzah's[82] body took Solomon's breath away. It seems to have been created

---

[80] Ryken, *Love of Loves in the Song of Songs*, 89.
[81] Ryken, *Love of Loves in the Song of Songs*, 89.
[82] Tirzah is the name Dillow and Pintus choose to refer to Solomon's wife.

from a very transparent fabric, because her adoring husband clearly described every part of her body, including her breasts and private "garden."[83]

Song of Solomon 4:12-15
A garden locked is my sister, my bride, a spring locked, a fountain sealed. Your shoots are an orchard of pomegranates with all choicest fruits, henna with nard, nard and saffron, calamus and cinnamon, with all trees of frankincense, myrrh and aloes, with all choice spices—a garden fountain, a well of living water, and flowing streams from Lebanon.

Solomon has cherished his gentle journey along his wife's body. He has arrived at the entrance gate to "her garden." What a beautifully poignant, yet deeply respectful way to refer to her vagina! When God chooses to use fruit and spices in His description, every woman realizes how much He values her body and the act of lovemaking. The scripture highlights the sacredness of the moment when Solomon asserts that the garden, the spring, the fountain are locked and sealed. Entrance was reserved for their wedding night. Ryken elaborates on the significance:

> Up until now, these two lovers have protected their purity. Rather than exploiting each other or experimenting with each other, as people often do in our permissive society, they had safeguarded their sexuality. This helps to explain why the groom compares his bride to a private garden.[84]

The focus of the images of a garden and a fountain shifts from representing the woman's virginal purity to her identity as the source of abundant and rich life. She is a luxuriant garden and a wall flowing with cool

---
[83] Dillow and Pintus, *Intimacy Ignited*, 150.
[84] Ryken, *Love of Loves in the Song of Songs*, 91.

streams of living water. What is being celebrated here is not perpetual virginity and abstinence, but rather a sexual purity that leads to and supports a fruitful and delightful union in marriage.[85]

Throughout this passion-filled journey, the bride and groom communicate. This is vitally important to remind your daughter that because God created us distinctively male and female, we are wired differently both emotionally and physiologically. A male's body is stimulated in different ways than a female body. Females are even more complicated than that because they respond differently, depending on the point in their monthly cycle and depending on their season of life and what happened that day. In order for a husband to understand what is pleasing to a wife, she must communicate. He needs clues. The Shulamite bride clued her husband in by praising and emphasizing the touch that was pleasurable to her. She kept the communication positive. We know she consistently stroked his body and passionately kissed him because Solomon praised her for her caresses. BUT sexual communication, especially words that name body parts, can sometimes be awkward. If you call body parts by their proper names, you feel like you are in bed with your gynecologist! If you choose terms that are slang, they may be understandable, but carry a connotation that feels dirty. We suggest newlyweds adopt their own love names for body parts or, better yet, follow the example of God and use phrases from His botanical creation. The important thing is that you encourage your daughter to lovingly and unashamedly communicate to her husband. He will appreciate the gentle reinforcement, and she will reap the benefits.

Throughout the *Song*, Shulamite warns her single friends, "*Do not awaken love,* until the wedding night. But, this time, in response to her groom, she sings, "Awake."

---

[85] Duguid, *Song of Songs,* 87.

Song of Solomon 4:16
Awake, O north wind, and come, O south wind! Blow upon my garden, let its spices flow.

The bride joins the poetic garden imagery by requesting that the north and south wind blow across her garden:

> In Palestine, the north wind brings clear weather and removes clouds, and the south wind brings warmth and moisture. When these winds blow across a garden, the combination of sun, rain and warmth promotes growth.[86]

Shulamite is encouraging Solomon to stimulate her "garden." Her husband has filled her with anticipation.

Song of Solomon 4:16c
Let my beloved come to his garden, and eat its choicest fruits.

When the bride's body is fully prepared, she invites her husband to enter the garden and enjoy to the max. According to 5:1, he does.

Song of Solomon 5:1
I came to my garden, my sister, my bride. I gathered my myrrh with my spice, I ate my honeycomb with my honey, I drank my wine with my milk.

Again, the wording here is the language of the Promised Land, a land flowing with milk and honey. Solomon repeatedly uses the possessive pronoun "my." He has received this gift from the Lord. The experience is every bit as exhilarating as he hoped.

Remember to explain to your daughter that the afterflow is an essential element of lovemaking. She should not just roll over and go to

---
[86] Dillow and Pintus, *Intimacy Ignited*, 152.

sleep, but rather savor the moment with her new husband. She can express to him how pleasurable it was to be so close and how thankful she is for him. This prepares the atmosphere with anticipation for their next sexual encounter.

I love this passage because it so powerfully illustrates the depth and intensity of combining covenant love, affectionate love, and sexual love. What an incredible bond! This is what your daughter longs for.

The groom and the bride both set self aside to intentionally concentrate on enhancing the relationship for the benefit of their covenant partner. The result was mutual ecstasy.

Remind your daughter that mutual ecstasy is a learning process that may or may not be fully realized on the wedding night. As they communicate and grow in understanding of one another's bodies and stimulation points, they will become more skilled. Orgasm is thrilling, but not the most important aspect of making love. God's intention is oneness, the melding of two into one emotionally, physically, and spiritually under the stability of covenant promises.

We agree with Duguid:

> The goal of the Song of Songs is not simply to teach God's people how to have great sex within marriage. Rather, the Song gives us a glimpse into the heart of the God who himself loves us so passionately. [87]

Only an unsurpassable passionate love could result in the sacrificial death on the cross for such an undeserving bride as us. The cross proves, "He didn't marry us because we were beautiful: he married us in order to make us beautiful by the power of his transforming love."[88]

His covenant love completely fulfills us. Encourage your daughter to strive to emulate that same covenant love in her relationship with her spouse. Our prayer is that when your daughter

---

[87] Duguid, *Song of Songs*, 92.
[88] Duguid, *Song of Songs*, 94.

marries, the truths will drive her to selflessly pursue her mate and to burn with desire for the perfect love relationship that can only be found in Christ.

Appendix A

Multiple Dating Relationships

Engaging in multiple dating relationships can encourage meaningless lust that grows stronger with each encounter. It also establishes negative patterns for attraction, then lust, then what? It is not healthy for anyone to reach the level of attachment (and the dreaded break-up) many times before they ever even consider marriage. This behavior, although completely acceptable by the world, trains our minds (and our hearts) to always keeps an exit plan available as an option. It becomes a tool that is used so often that it is completely natural to expect it could be used at any time in the future when relationships are not what we expected.

An alternative option would be to approach relationships in group settings rather than dating exclusively. Here singles can observe character and narrow the choices of potential mates with an intent to discover whether a particular person is suited for marriage before they ever begin a relationship. They can also include activities with family that reveal how the potential mate fits their concept of marriage. We recommend reading *When God Writes Your Love Story* by Eric and Leslie Ludy.

Character Considerations in a Future Mate

Genuine Christianity: The most important character consideration in a future mate is whether that person is a child of God. This is not just an important consideration, but an actual warning with instruction from God.

> *Do not be unequally yoked with unbelievers. For what partnership has righteousness with lawlessness? Or what fellowship has light with darkness? 2 Corinthians 6:14*

Merely claiming Christianity is not enough proof of genuine relationship with Christ. The prospective mate should exhibit passion for Jesus and His truth. Going to church and saying, "I am a Christian" is not enough evidence that one's identity is in Christ. So, how can we recognize this in someone?

The conversation of a Christian should show an awe of God, a respect for His Word, a dependency on His power, and what He has done on the cross. I lose count of the husbands and wives seeking counsel for shipwrecked marriages that sit in our living room and declare, "I thought she was a Christian…I thought he was a believer of Christ." The strategic time for concern about a spouse's walk with God is before the relationship begins. Ask your daughter if she can pinpoint examples of spiritual depth in the guy she is considering. Can he talk about something besides cars, sports, or food? Is there some spiritual depth to the person?

Kindness: I advise teen girls to pay attention to how a guy treats his mother and how he interacts with his sister because when he gets used to her, that is how he will eventually treat her.

Honesty: If a guy will lie to his parents or his supervisor, eventually he will deceive his girlfriend or wife. If a guy cheats on a test, eventually he will cheat on you. These habits are directly linked to character. If they exist, they will manifest in married life. Nothing strains a relationship like distrust.

Work Ethic: Does the prospective mate exhibit a strong work ethic? Marriage requires teamwork. Laziness stresses marriage. A husband without a respectable work ethic will struggle to provide for his family. A wife who shies away from the effort of work will struggle to balance the requirements of motherhood and responsibilities in the home. Man's work and woman's relationships were cursed (*Genesis* 3:14-19) making it even more important that they seek God's help living out their God-given roles.

Confirming integrity and character require much observation. Getting to know someone is a process that should occur long before entering a relationship. Hanging out with friends in a group, participating in group activities, attending Bible Studies with discussion opportunities, and observing responses to stress and challenges are the most fertile ground for discerning genuine surrender to Christ.

A mom can begin highlighting desirable traits at an early age by offering praise for others during daily conversation. "Your friend happily shares her toys." "That girl works hard and is quick to offer a helping hand." "He always consoles people who are sad." "What a generous act!" "That's the kind of people we like to hang out with."

Conquering Insecurities

Voicing insecurities is a form of self-absorption and can become consuming to the point that it is unattractive and hinders successful lovemaking.

I remember a sweet bride-to-be who came to me privately. She was genuinely concerned that on her wedding night, when her husband saw a particular aspect of her unclothed body, he would be repulsed. This is a very real concern. Because I personally knew the groom and how he loved her for who she was rather than how she looked, I was able to reassure her that he would not allow her flaw to interfere with their intimacy. Her beauty was more than skin deep, but she needed more than my reassurance. She needed to know how to combat the nagging worry.

Solomon's bride experienced a similar dilemma because she failed to meet the cultural standard of beauty (*Song of Solomon* 1:5-6). Rather than obsess over her inadequacies, Solomon's fiancé chose to do the following:

1. Recognize her negative thinking.
2. Acknowledge the positive aspects of what she had to offer her husband (*Philippians* 4:8).
3. Intentionally shift her attention to concentrate on pleasing her groom. As you saw in the epilogue, on their wedding night, Solomon repeatedly expressed specific gratitude for her sexual skill.

The advice must have been effective because I just saw on Facebook that the young lady who came to me is happily married with three children.

There was also a time, when my four sons were high school and college age, I was preparing to speak to high school girls about purity. I had my guys sit down on the sofa and tell me what they found attractive in girls. One of my sons was eager to tell what interested him; but first, he was going to share what turned him off! He went on to say when a girl walked around with her shoulders slumped and talked about how ugly she was, he found the attitude repelling. He was impressed with girls that were comfortable with who God made them to be, not girls who obsessed over inadequacies. He was attracted to the girls who displayed confidence in the Lord. Solomon was impressed with his bride's confidence that was displayed in her queenly posture.

Appendix A

You may ask how do I become comfortable with who God made me to be?

1. Rather than boosting self-confidence which leads to arrogance, increase God-confidence by studying the attributes of God and allowing yourself to become fascinated with His character. Resource: *The God You Can Know* by Dan DeHaan
2. Embrace your identity in Christ. Resource: *Face Time: Your Identity in a Selfie World,* by Kristen Hatton (A must read for every female single.)

Appendix B

Release from Sexual Bondage

Resources:
- *Rid of My Disgrace* by Holcomb
- *The Secret Thoughts of an Unlikely Convert* by Rosaria Butterfield.
- *Gentle and Lowly* by Dane Ortlund
- *Redemption* by Mark Wilkerson

Appendix C

Living It Out in the Home

Along with proper biblical explanation, faithfully loving our spouse in front of our children, establishes healthy anticipation for married life while fueling a desire for purity before marriage.

Submission

God's design for the home is grace-filled teamwork where the husband assumes the role of the coach who discusses "plays" with his wife-coordinator. She should expect and allow him to make final game-plan decisions that promote the good of the family. The wife-coordinator offers perspective, but follows the husband-coach's game plan.

Both you and your daughter should pursue a scriptural understanding of a husband's servant-like leadership and a wife's devoted submission. We have found value in reading many trustworthy books on marriage and the wife's role. Not only does this help a concerned mom to model God's plan as an example for her daughter, but it also encourages our daughters to read books together with us to prepare her heart. It also enables her to recognize the leadership qualities to watch for in a perspective husband.

Suggested Resources:

- *Feminine Appeal* by Carolyn Mahaney
- *The Excellent Wife* by Martha Peace
- *Helper by God's Design* by Elyse Fitzpatrick

Appendix D

Mother-Daughter Activities

Bonding was not all together a natural occurrence for my oldest daughter and me. Neither of us was to blame. Our personalities and dispositions required us to work for it. It was definitely a learned skill.

I sought out ideas for encouraging this mother-daughter bond that we needed help to develop. I deeply desired a connection that would allow us to freely share our weighty thoughts, ambitious dreams, and spiritual insight. What I found to work was not a plug and play system. What drove us closer together were heavy prayers and grace.

By "heavy," I mean those prayers that cause you to wrestle with your flesh. For example, when the Spirit directs you to pray and immediately, warfare begins, then you have to be determined to battle through to the end. I'm talking about those prayers that you hesitate to pray because the Spirit has already revealed that the answer may be unpleasant. As uncomfortable as they truly are, the time spent praying in this manner is truly the most rewarding to our relationship.

I have found that being a parent forces me to come face to face with the worst of myself in order to direct my children in the way I know the Lord would have them go. All the while, facing the realization that His plan for them is also His plan for me. Grace has a way of entering into a conversation and taking us back in time. I can be approached by my daughter in need of advice; and at the same time that I am trying to disciple her, grace reminds me of my need.

My daughter responds best to observing my passion rather than being provided with instructions that she should follow. It is much easier for me to hand out specific advice including rules and guidelines. Living out my faith in front of her takes intentionality and time. Up until age 9, I had unsuccessfully chosen to go head-to-head with her. I had a strong desire to control her with the hope of also directing her future and keeping her safe. In His kindness, God gently broke me and redirected my approach back to grace.

Our greatest bonding emerges from our time together in God's word. She chooses to emulate my time alone with God as she has witnessed the strength it has provided me in very dark times. When she sees the joy and encouragement that I receive from gathering with a group of ladies for Bible study, she, too, is motivated to join us or even better, start one herself! I once received an invaluable piece of advice when I asked, "How do I teach my children to love the Lord?" "You live passionately for the Lord. Your children will be passionate about what you are passionate about."

I love encouraging moms to share their passion for the Lord with their daughters with these ideas:

Mother-Daughter Journal: I started writing to my daughter when she was young. I don't write entries as often as I would like, but I do try to be intentional about what I am able to write. I have a Bible that I plan to give her, along with the journal, when she turns eighteen. Each entry focuses on a godly trait that she has exhibited or a wise choice she has made with the help of the Holy Spirit. I always include scripture to affirm her actions and her character. I mark these specific scriptures in her Bible for her future reference.

Memorizing Scripture: We began memorizing scripture together early in her childhood, but we have allowed distractions to interfere as she has aged and as our family has grown. I do desire to reinstate this as a practice for our entire family. The impact that scripture can have on the lives of our children is simply invaluable.

Bible Studies: We hosted a study just for girls ages 9-12 one summer. It was birthed from the very Bible Study that Debbie and I had with moms to discuss how to talk with our daughters about sex. Macy saw women coming to our home to study the Bible, and she said she wished she could do the same with girls her age. So, we did! Bible studies are a great way to enliven their personal faith in God.

Baking a Cake: Macy has always enjoyed being in the kitchen as well as dreaming of being a competitor in a baking competition on television. As we watched a series together, we were reminded that following instructions can be to our benefit. If we choose to bake a cake simply by throwing all of the ingredients in a bowl (without following a recipe), it will taste gross. However, if we use all of the right ingredients AND follow the recipe correctly, it will taste yummy! This is the same for following God's plan, or recipe, for sex!

Conversation: There is no greater way to bond with your daughter than to listen. I am still learning this skill. When I am too quick to share advice, I'm learning to apologize and confess my need to listen. More recently, I found myself asking her to let me know when she is looking for advice. Otherwise, I plan to listen without judgment first.

Appendix E

Awaken Resources

- *Intended For Pleasure* by Ed Wheat who is a Christian medical doctor and sex therapist.
- www.PreparingforPartnership.org is an online premarital course preparing couples for the lifelong journey of Christian marriage. Lesson Six expounds the material from this appendix so that both male and female will increase their understanding of the details God provides for lovemaking.
- *A Loving Life* by Paul Miller teaches the power of selfless covenant love and how to embrace it for marriage.

Visit the author, Amanda Clark's website at www.disciplingwomen.com

And on social media at:

SERVANT_TO_THESAINTS

Divine Appointments

Servant_to_thesaints

Author's Other Works:

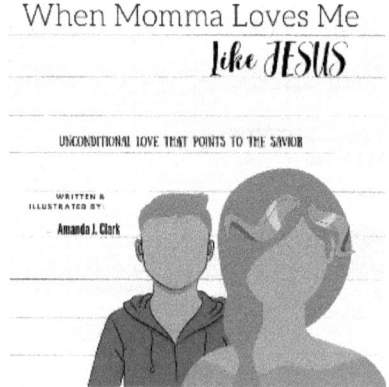

Visit the author, Debbie Wood's ministry website at www.familyfortress.org and on social media.

FAMILY FORTRESS ministries

 familyfortress

 Family Fortress Ministries

 @familyfortress

Author's Other Works:

PREPARING *for* PARTNERSHIP

Preparing for Partnership is an online premarital training course for engaged couples. The site allows participants to individually take lessons at their own pace in the privacy of their home. The program is designed using Biblical principles as a guideline in each instructional lesson. Lessons include "Readiness", "Covenant", "Companionship", "Communication", Resolving Conflict, Sexual intimacy, "Roles & Responsibilities", "Finances", "Children" and much more. Provision is made to include a pastor or facilitator to monitor the progress of the couples if so desired.

Marriage is the most important decision in your life; however, many times couples spend more time and energy planning the wedding day than they do preparing for their life together. With the limited amount of time that current schedules allow, Preparing for Partnership provides a way to effectively prepare for marriage so that your relationship will be a lifelong, fulfilling commitment of true love.

www.preparingforpartnership

www.ingramcontent.com/pod-product-compliance
Lightning Source LLC
Chambersburg PA
CBHW070201100426
42743CB00013B/2999